In 1980 something happened that had never occurred before through the span of four and a half million millennia. On January 1, 1980, the first member of the Millennial Generation or Generation Y was born. While that event passed with no more notice than the birth of any child, it meant that exactly 18 years later we would live in a world different from anything we had known before.

For the first time in history, there are now four generations of adults living, working and learning within the same society. It sets a tone for the explosion of change that society faces in the 21st century.

For the first time, there are four generations of adults raising families, going to work, going to school. The day of the multi-age classroom is here. The issues of how to manage diverse generations in the workplace are upon us.

Generational Learning Styles is a pioneering work intended to provide you with guidelines for meeting the challenges of multiple generations in school, work and society.

For trainers, teachers at all levels, faculty, human resource professionals and anyone interested in generations and in learning styles. After reading *Generational Learning Styles*, you will be more creative and successful in your own teaching and work.

Generational Learning Styles

by Julie Coates

Published by LERN Books, a division of
Learning Resources Network (LERN)
P.O. Box 9
River Falls, Wisconsin 54022
U.S.A.

Phone: 800-678-5376 (US and Canada)
E-mail: *info@lern.org*
URL: *www.lern.org*

Manufactured in the United States of America

5   4   3   2   1

Library of Congress Cataloging in Publication Data
Coates, Julie, 1946-
  Generational Learning Styles

ISBN 1-57722-032-3

Acknowledgments

I am indebted to many people who have made contributions to this book. First, I would like to thank my sons, Jason Coates and Willie Draves, for inspiring me to explore the differences in how members of younger generations learn and communicate their learning. I am also grateful to my mother-in-law, Alice Draves, for her insights into the G. I. Generation, and to my father, Y. A. Taylor, who, as a teacher and a member of the G. I. Generation, as well, provided through both example and instruction, a wealth of information about what it means to be an effective teacher and to reach learners across the lifespan. I wish to thank my mother, Helen Taylor, for her faith in me and for her unrelenting commitment to education as a cornerstone for success for her children.

For the cover photographs, I would like to than Greg "Grease" Lehman for both his fine example of body art and for permission to use the photograph of his work. I also wish to thank Allen Garcie, Graphic Design & Marketing Coordinator, Division of Continuing Education and Public Service at Louisiana State University in Shreveport, for permission to use the photograph of Severn B. Doughty, Jr., the young WWII GI, and Devin Wiley, a member of Generation Y, for permission to use his photograph with his cell phone on the cover of this book. The picture of the Baby Boomer is the author at age 23, photograph by Gary Coates.

I am dependent upon and grateful to all the staff at LERN for their help and support in this project. Debbie Barron was very helpful in providing assistance with information gathering. Rebel Rush, Gale Hughes and Tammy Peterson have provided support, feedback and encouragement throughout the writing process. John Allen, I thank for helping me keep a sense of humor and for periodic reality checks. In particular, I would like to thank Nancy Hulverson for her careful editing and proof-reading of the final manuscript, for her insightful comments and suggestions, and for her assistance in acquiring permission for use of quotations and photographs used in this volume. To Jason Coates, my thanks for advice and assistance with graphic design decisions and consultation on the cover design. Also, I want to thank Christopher Olson for his assistance with proof-reading and production of the final manuscript, and Danita Dickinson for her extreme competence and professionalism in production. With such strong support from so many talented people, it should be obvious to all that any errors contained in this book are solely the responsibility of the author.

To my colleagues Paul Franklin, Julia King Tamang, Kassia Dellabough, and Greg Marsello, thank you for your support and enthusiasm for this effort, and to Suzanne Kart, my thanks for substantive input on the mysterious workings of Generation X.

Finally, I would like to thank my husband and colleague, William Draves, for his support and encouragement, and for his gentle nudging when this project fell behind schedule. Without his assistance, feedback, counsel, and insight, this book would never have come into being.

Dedication

To Helen and Y. A. Taylor,
the greatest parents in the Greatest Generation.

Generational Learning Styles

Table of Contents

Introduction   1

Chapter 1: Who are the Generations?   5

Chapter 2: Some Thoughts on Learning Theory   9

Chapter 3: A Brief History of Pedagogy in the 20th Century   19

Chapter 4: Learning and the Brain   27

Chapter 5: Culture and Community in a Changing Society   41

Chapter 6: Generations and Social Change   49

Chapter 7: The Cohort Experience   61

Chapter 8: The Veterans (1920-1945)   63

Chapter 9: Veterans and Silents in the Classroom   81

Chapter 10: Baby Boomers (1946-1964)   83

Chapter 11: Generation X (1965-1980)   91

Chapter 12: Generation Y (1980-2000)   111

Chapter 13: A Pedagogy for the 21st Century   129

References   139

Bibliography   146

About LERN   148

For More About Generational Learning Styles   149

Introduction

Most scientists accept that the age of the earth is about 4.5 billion years, but in 1980, something happened that had never occurred before through the span of four and a half million millennia. On January 1, 1980, the first member of the Millennial Generation or Generation Y was born, and while that event passed with no more notice than the birth of any child, it meant that exactly 18 years later we would live in a world different from anything we had known before. For the first time in history, in 1998, there were four generations of adults living, working, and learning within the same society. This has never occurred before in our history, and it sets a tone for the explosion of change that society faces in the 21st century. For the first time, there are four generation of adults raising families, going to work, going to school. The day of the multi-age classroom is here, and the issues of how to manage diverse generations in the workplace are upon us. This book is intended to provide some guidance in meeting those challenges.

These are times like no others. It is possible to sit on a park bench in some cities and communicate via wireless Internet connections with people around the globe. Grandparents can view their newly born grandchild online within hours of its birth. Young people can maintain relationships with friends in many countries and from a wide range of cultures. Technology has changed the world.

On a more mundane level, a high school dropout with access to the Internet can access the formula for finding the area of a pyramid in order to use the information to construct a box for his car stereo. Youth at risk can learn about probability by researching the sexual behavior of Genghis Khan or, out of curiosity, determine the volume of a newly constructed water tank for their community.

These changes in the nature of information and the availability of information are staggering, but they are further complicated by the demographic changes that have occurred at the end of the 20th and beginning of the 21st centuries. Not only are there more people, but there are more adults in every age cohort. For the first time in history, educators and trainers are faced with teaching and training adults whose ages range from their late teens and early twenties to their eighties. Such a range of ages has never been common in the classrooms, training rooms and workplaces of the past, and this demographic reality presents new challenges to educators, trainers and managers. As the retirement age moves toward age 70, it is likely that there will be an increasing number of older adults in the classroom and the workplace. It is essential that educators and managers learn the skills to teach and manage effectively in an age-diverse world.

This book is a tool for to help meet this challenge. It contains information on each generation, with practical strategies to improve both teaching and communication across the generations.

The information provided here is intended to guide you to a better understanding of how to successfully teach students of different ages. The goal is to provide you with information that you can use to understand the outlook and context within which people of different generations approach learning, so that you can be more creative and successful in your own teaching.

Keep in mind that every individual is different. That does not, however, mean that it is impossible for people with certain shared cultural experiences to develop similar sets of behaviors and outlooks. As much as we are individuals, we also share much in common with our peers. Thus, if we assert that baby boomers are avid learners, it does not mean that *every* baby boomer is an avid learner. We all know individuals who are baby boomers and who are not at all interested in pursuing additional learning opportunities.

It means that, statistically, baby boomers are more likely to engage in learning activities than their predecessors, and/or that more baby boomers are likely to pursue independent learning interests than other groups, or that a significant number of adults in this category say that learning and education are important to them, etc.

Likewise, if we say that Millenials are more likely to have good manners than Gen Xers, it does not mean that all Millenials are polite or that all Gen Xers are rude. It simply means that certain behaviors are more typical of each group than of others. I raise this point because I do not wish any of you to become frustrated when we must, for the purposes of discussion, make certain broad characterizations. This is unavoidable, and I encourage you to remember that our broad statements are based on behaviors that have been analyzed and measured for statistically significant presence among population groups.

To fully understand the implications of societal change upon generations and upon learning preferences, it is necessary to consider a wide array of forces that impinge upon people's lives, and how these forces change with time. In order to understand these better, we will explore a variety of cultural phenomena including social, economic, demographic, technological, and scientific, as well as educational — for it is the collective influence of all these societal forces that results in the changes across generations that are the focus of this book.

Chapter 1: Who are the Generations?

There is debate about this question. The baby boom earned its name when the birth rate soared above 3.5 million per year in the United States and above 4 million for several years. The Baby Bust (more commonly called Generation X) was that cohort that followed the Baby Boom. While many demographers and marketers have different definitions of just what years comprise each generation, in this book the definition will be based on birth rate.

It is absolutely the case that there is wide variation within each generation, and that members of generational cohorts are not social, philosophical, educational, or economic clones of each other. It is also true that generations tend to merge into each other so that the youngest Baby Boomers may have more in common with Generation Xers than with leading edge Boomers. In fact, because of this very phenomenon, we have Generation Jones. This segment of the Baby Boom generation was named by Johathan Pontell, now in his mid-forties. It applies to that segment of boomers (the largest segment, by the way) born between 1954 and 1965. Numbering about 53 million, it represents about seventy-five percent of the total Boomer population (Williams, 2002).

"Too young to be a Boomer and too old to be a Gen Xer," Pontell created a new generation. Undeniably a part of the Baby Boom, Generation Jones represents a quintessentially Boomer philosophy... make yourself different, keep yourself young, make yourself stand out from the crowd. This reality reflects the importance of acknowledging both

5

major values and trends that tend to exist within generations while also demonstrating that change is constantly occurring and evolving. Further, it illustrates quite profoundly that there are segments and sub-segments of every cohort. The intent of this book is not to examine the minute psychographic changes that occur within generational cohorts, but rather to explore the major consistencies in values and behavior that guide larger societal trends.

Using this principle as a guideline, we define the generations as follows. Note that the two oldest generations were names "after the fact," i.e., until we began naming the generations with the Boomers, there was no name to identify generational shifts.

- **The Veteran Generation** — 1920-1933 (WWII Veterans, larger cohort)
- **The Silent Generation** — 1933-1946 (Depression babies, smaller cohort)
- **Baby Boom** — 1946-1964 (birth rate above 3.5 million/year to 4 million/year)
- **Generation X** — 1964-1980 (birth rate below 3.5 million/year)
- **Generation Y** — 1980-2000* (birth rate above 3.5 million to 4 million/year)
- **Generation Z** — 2000+ (birth rate consistently above 4 million/year)

The chart on the following page provides a graphic image of the population distribution in the United States in 2000. The Baby Boom is clearly evident as the large bulge in the middle of the chart. Generation X is the smaller cohort just below the bulge, and Generation Y can be seen as the numbers within younger cohort increases. It is interesting to note that the population of older adults is growing — and that as it ages, the population becomes increasingly female.

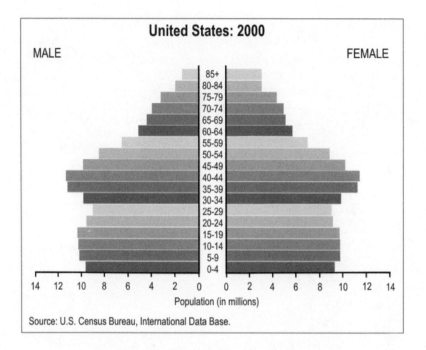

United States: 2000

MALE   FEMALE

Source: U.S. Census Bureau, International Data Base.

By 2025, the population will begin to look quite different. The Baby Boomers will be well into their retirement years, and while their numbers will still be large, they will comprise an overall smaller percentage of the total population. This demonstrates how generational/age diversity is here to stay, and that developing communication, management, and teaching tools to address this demographic reality are something that must happen now. If we look at the demographic profile projected for 2050, this becomes even more apparent. Into the middle of the century and beyond, we will be teaching in age-diverse classrooms.

By 2050, the population pyramid will look like the population beehive. The youngest Baby Boomers will be in their mid to late 80s and age segmentation will be a constant in society, rather than a novel situation to which society must adjust.

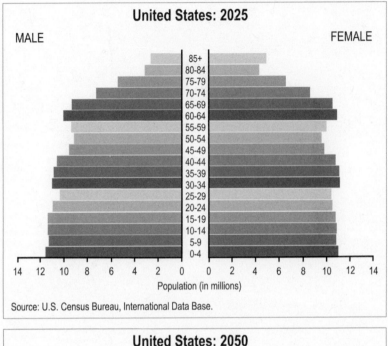

Source: U.S. Census Bureau, International Data Base.

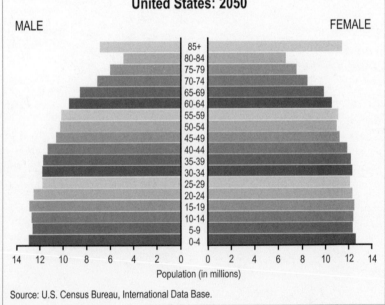

Source: U.S. Census Bureau, International Data Base.

Chapter 2: Some Thoughts on Learning Theory

What is learning style?

The efforts of humans to understand how learning happens date back to 427 BC when Plato and Socrates philosophized on the origin of knowledge. However, it was not until 1954, when Herb Thelan coined the term "learning style" that there began to be substantial research dealing with the differences in how learners process information (Hicks and Gable, 1999).

We will begin our investigation of the generational aspects of learning style with a brief overview of the literature on learning styles and on how this concept has been incorporated into the pedagogy of the last century. The broadest definition of learning style is a "student's consistent way of responding to and using stimuli in the context of learning" (Claxon and Ralston, 1978). Rezler and Rezmovic (1981) stated "learning style is the manner in which an individual perceives and processes information in learning situations." Regardless of the exact definition, there is substantial evidence that individuals have different ways of learning, and that these are influenced by how an individual experiences the world.

Recent research has shown that students are characterized by significantly different learning styles. Individuals screen information through a set of unique, individual filters. They manipulate information in different ways, and they achieve understanding at different rates within different contexts (Felder, 1993). Research also shows that the nature of the teaching environment has a profound impact upon the ability of students to learn. Sheila Tobias (1990), in her research on how students performed in introductory science classes at the college level, found that by changing the way they structured a class and how they presented information, teachers could create substantial variations of success among students.

In the past twenty years, there has been a growing awareness that cultural experiences and life experiences influence behavior, work and learning. A lot of the research in this area has focused on behavior at work and in the training setting. Increasingly, trainers have become aware that there are substantial generational differences, not only in attitudes about work, but in attitudes about learning and in preferences for how learning takes place (Zemke, et. al., 2000). While most of the research on learning styles deals with cognitive, behavioral or psychological styles, the age diversity in today's classrooms demands that educators give attention to the generational issues that affect how students learn and how effectively they learn.

Before turning to the generational issues, it is important that we look first at some of the traditional research on learning styles. We have to remember that even with generational differences, cognitive, behavioral, and psychological factors are still at play. They may simply manifest differently within different generations.

Learning Style Models

There have been many researchers of learning styles, and a variety of learning style models have been developed. Among those most commonly used are:

Felder-Silverman Learning Style Model
This model classifies students as:
- Sensing (concrete, practical, oriented toward facts and procedures) or Intuitive (conceptual, innovative, oriented toward theories/meanings)
- Inductive (prefer presentations that proceed from specific to general) or
  Deductive (prefer presentations that go from the general to the specific)

- Active (learn by trying things out, working with others) or Reflective (learn by thinking things through, working alone)
- Sequential (linear, orderly, learn in small incremental steps) or Global (holistic, systems thinkers, learn in large leaps)

Gardner's Theory of Multiple Intelligences

Gardner originally asserted that there are seven "intelligences," and that it is possible to be gifted with one type of intelligence and to be very unsuccessful in another type. He has recently added an eighth intelligence — Natural Learner. The original seven include: Linguistic Learner, Logical/Mathematical Learner, Spatial Learner, Musical Learner, Bodily Kinesthetic Learner, Interpersonal Learner, and Intra-personal Learner. The eighth intelligence, Natural Learner, is the ability to observe, interpret, and construct meaning from the natural world (Gardner, 1993).

Gregorc Learning Style Indicator

Anthony Gregorc developed a model that focuses on random and sequential processing of information. This is similar to "top-down" and "bottom-up" processing. Top-down learners look at the whole task (random) while bottom-up learners look at the information a step at a time (sequential).

Hermann Brain Dominance Instrument (HBDI)

This model classifies students in terms of their relative preferences for thinking in four different modes based on how the brain handles specialized tasks. The four modes in this model are:
- Quadrant A: Left Brain, Cerebral (Logical, analytical, quantitative, factual, critical)
- Quadrant B: Left Brain, Limbic (Sequential, organized, planned, detailed, structured)
- Quadrant C: Right Brain, Limbic (Emotional, interpersonal, sensory, kinesthetic, symbolic
- Quadrant D: Right Brain Cerebral (Visual, holistic, innovative)

Kolb Learning Style Model

This model classifies students as having a preference for concrete experience or abstract conceptualization (how they take information in), and active experimentation or reflective observation (how they internalize information). This model allows for four learning style types.

Long/Dzuiban Learning Style Inventory

This inventory, developed by Dr. William Long, is a developmental model based on dimensions of aggressive/passive and dependence/independence. The theory was derived from his observations of ambivalence expressed by adolescents as they progressed developmentally from a state of dependence to independence. The four types of patterns identified by this model include:

1. Aggressive-Independent (high energy, action oriented, risk takers, leaders)
2. Aggressive-Dependent (high energy, but direct energy toward gaining approval, superior intellect, interact closely with teachers, participate in class, leaders, self-critical)
3. Passive-Independent (stubborn, withdraw or become inactive when stressed, don't participate in class, control over authority is a primary goal)
4. Passive-Dependent (low energy, thrive on affection and approval, extremely sensitive, do more than required, kind, gentle)

Meyers-Briggs Type Indicator (MBTI)

This model classifies students according to their preferences on scales derived from Carl Jung's theory of psychological types. Type preferences can be combined to form 16 different learning style types.

The models listed above are by no means all of the Models, Indices, Indicators and Scales that have been developed and researched in the effort to understand the process of how thinking and learning occurs. In fact, some 30 theories of learning styles and more than 30 instruments for evaluating learning styles have been put forward (Ouellette, 2000). In reviewing these various assessment tools, it is apparent that they measure a variety of different aspects of human function. Some measure *learning preferences* - how someone chooses to work and the kind of environment they prefer. Others measure *cognitive styles* — whether someone focuses on details or the big picture. Others look at personality type such as introverted/extroverted or aggressive/passive. Still others, such as Gardner's theory of multiple intelligences, look at learning from the perspective of aptitude theory of multiple intelligences. The National Association of School Principals (NAASP) set up a Learning Style Task Force that combined previous learning style models and extracted their version through factor analysis. They defined learning style as "the consistent pattern of behavior and performance by which an individual approaches educational experiences." It is the composite of characteristic cognitive, affective, and physiological behaviors that are relatively stable indicators of how a learner perceives, interacts with, and responds to the learning environment." (National Task Force on Learning Style, 1979). The model is composed of three styles: 1) cognitive, 2) affective, and 3) physiological. The Task Force contended that other existing models only address one or two of those styles. They also developed a computer-scored learning style inventory for secondary school students.

All is not complete chaos, however, as most of these assessment instruments are based on developing two fundamental dimensions of cognitive style that incorporate holistic vs. analytic thinking and verbal vs. visual thinking (Ouellette, 2000). Many of the learning styles identified by these assessment tools use different terminology, categories, and combinations of style, making for a very dynamic set of options for analysis of learning styles.

When, in 1956, Bruner, Goodnow, and Austin introduced the concept of learning styles in their research, "A Study of Thinking," the idea took hold that it was possible to know how people know. From that time until now, there has been a gradual revolution in how educators think about the learning process. It has shifted from a behaviorist, mechanistic view "that learning is a simple, reflexive and quantifiable activity" to the active and organistic notion that "learners have organized knowledge bases and actively participate in the construction of their reality" (Tessmer and Jonassen, 1988).

In looking ahead to some of the characteristics of those who grew up between 1950 and 1980, we will probably not be surprised to learn that it was during those years the idea emerged that "learning styles" could be measured, defined and linked to instructional styles that would enhance learning. As we will discover during the course of our study, it was during the decades of the 1950s and 1960s that there emerged a profound confidence and belief that science could and would explain everything. Boomers grew up believing that, unless something could be quantitatively measured and explained, it was of necessity bogus. It was the age of logical positivism when any "unexplainable" phenomenon was seen as charlatanism and anything that could not be proven empirically was suspect.

It is no wonder, then, that people in the 1950s and 1960s not only believed that it was possible to quantify, measure, explain and apply definitions of learning styles to every individual, but that learning styles were relatively static and did not change over time. Even in current research, there is the assertion that "learning styles do not change."

That kind of thinking has led to a possible over-emphasis on the idea that "we are how we learn." Recently, the Meyers Briggs Personality Inventory was administered to my eighth grade son and his fellow students. For several days, students walked through the halls of their middle school with badges that declared them to be "ENTP" or "INTJ" or whatever. It is not uncommon for these students to remark, since the inventory was administered, that "I will have trouble with this because I am an "ISFJ." The profiles and assessments were never intended to "lock" students into specific categories, although there is a tendency among both students and teachers to accept the outcomes of Meyers Briggs and other assessments as definitive. Such measures are simply intended to identify preferences that have an influence on how people learn and interact within their environment. While there is a great deal of research and general acceptance of learning style theory, almost unanimously, researchers report that the best learning occurs when teachers "teach to all learning styles." There are few, if any, studies that have been able to clearly document that matching teaching and learning styles, at least with children, results in improved learning on the part of students.

This is not to denigrate the value of learning style identification, nor to suggest that there is no value in having teachers who are sensitive to the learning style preferences of their students. It does suggest, however, that there is something more at play than just learning style preferences as they have traditionally been viewed. Felder and Silverman (1988) note that in a study of university students, there was a clear tendency for students in Engineering to show a similar learning style preference, i.e., abstract, intuitive, passive and sequential. This type of research suggests that there are certain learning preferences and skills that may lead to success in specific areas of study. This does not mean, however that all successful Engineers are abstract, intuitive, passive and sequential learners — merely that this particular style of learning may lead students into scientific study.

One key issue that begs for examination is that of the interplay between environment and learning preferences that may influence the ways in which students learn most efficiently. In her book, *How to Implement and Supervise a Learning Style Program (1996)* Rita Dunn includes discussion of the importance of the physical environment as part of the mix necessary to provide a responsive learning situation.

As you walk into a classroom designed to facilitate Dunn's learning styles approach to instruction, you will notice visible and obvious characteristics. The physical arrangement of the classroom and the general atmosphere are unique. "Learning styles" classrooms have a mixture of furniture and equipment arranged differently from the typical classroom with rows of student desks. The furniture configuration usually includes one or more tables that will accommodate small groups of students. Individual student desks will also be seen, but their arrangement depends on the particular classroom. In other areas of the room, you may see easy chairs and/or carpets and lounging cushions. Although somewhat controversial, Dunn's models have been incorporated broadly into both public and private schools.

One interesting aspect of the Dunn model is that it incorporates five different types of preferences — environmental, emotional, sociological, physiological, and psychological (cognitive processing) preferences:

- Environmental Stimuli Preferences (sound, light, temperature, design)
- Emotional Stimuli Preferences (motivation, persistence, responsibility, and structure)
- Sociological Preferences (self, pair, peers/team, adult, varied)
- Physiological Stimuli Preferences (perceptual, intake, time, mobility)
- Psychological Stimuli Preferences (global/analytic style, hemisphericity, impulsive/reflective)

If we accept that each of these five stimuli categories comprises an aspect of the effectiveness of the learning environment and the effectiveness with which students learn, it is even more likely that we will find substantial differences in the preferred methods of learning among different age groups. In particular, the sociological and psychological stimuli preferences are of interest.

Patterns and preferences established on the basis of life experiences

Two Visual Learners
Two INTJ's

*The author and her son have very similar
learning styles but learn very differently.*

may, in fact, have a larger impact on how people prefer to learn than we
have considered.

Malcolm Knowles (1973), the Father of Adult Education, developed
his theory of Andragogy to explain the differences between how adults
and children learn. Although Knowles did not use the terminology "learning styles," many of the characteristics of andragogy could be translated
into "learning styles" terminology. If, in fact, adults and children do learn
in fundamentally different ways, it is reasonable that we might:

a. Expect that learning styles do change over time, with experience
and with learning task.

b. Expect that younger adults might learn best in ways that differ from
the ways in which children and older adults learn most efficiently.

c. Expect that environment and experience may have an impact on how
people prefer to learn and how efficiently they are able to learn.

Context and Learning Style

One obvious truth about all the learning style indicators is that everyone will fit into one of a limited number of definitions. Regardless of whether the respondent is 15 years old or 75 years old, he or she will "fit" into a category of learning styles based on the attributes the particular assessment is intended to measure. However, one must wonder whether a 75-year-old who shows a strong preference for "visual learning" will learn in the same way as a 15-year-old who shows a strong preference for "visual learning." Teachers observe differences among different cohorts of students, and these differences, generational based, are the focus of this book.

Learning style indicators are very valuable tools for educators. Increasingly, it is important to address differences in how individuals learn, and help students maximize their academic success. However, learning styles, as they have traditionally been viewed, are only one part of the puzzle that helps teachers understand how to bring out the best in their students. Experience, culture, values, and societal expectations are all part of the complex set of factors that influence how students learn best.

As society evolves in response to the changes in demographics, technology, and political forces that contribute to the development of 21st century culture, how we learn and what we need to learn will change as well. New competencies required in our contemporary world will demand different content and teaching styles to adequately help students acquire and master the skills needed to be successful in the world of the 21st century.

Our schools, so efficient in educating the workforce for the industrial era, must re-tool to provide the education that is required now, in the new era of information and technology. Understanding how today's students learn, and understanding how generational values affect both teaching and learning, will become increasingly important to assure that students receive quality education which prepares them for success in the 21st century.

Chapter 3: A Brief History of Pedagogy in the 20ᵗʰ Century

"School Days, School Days, dear old golden rule days,
Readin' and 'ritin' and 'rithmetic,
Taught to the tune of a hick'ry stick..."
— *Lyrics by Will Cobb, Music by Gus Edwards*

This familiar old song, writtenIntroduction in 1907 by Will Cobb, provides a succinct and descriptive summary of much of 20ᵗʰ century pedagogy. As society moved from an economy based on agriculture to an economy based on the factory, the role of education also began to shift. While school had been an option, and often a luxury in the 1800s, it became a necessity for a society that needed to produce workers who could function successfully in the factory, and to socialize large immigrant populations that streamed to America at the turn of the 20ᵗʰ century. In response to this rapid change in society, schools began to take on the challenge of educating and socializing students to succeed in an industrial economy.

By 1918, every state in America had passed a compulsory education law, which required that students attend school every year between the ages of 7 and 16 (America at School). As more and more young people entered formal education, educators worked to develop strategies and models to provide the most education to the most people in the most efficient manner. In 1900, according to U.S. census data, only about half of eligible students were enrolled in school, and, on average, received only about five years of education. From 1900 to 2000, the percentage of teenagers who graduated from high school increased from about 6 percent to about 88 percent. Only about 17 percent of children in the United States had a high school education in 1900, but by 1920, the number had more than doubled to 35 percent (U.S. Census Bureau, 1999).

The Progressive Education Movement

One hundred years ago, at the beginning of the 20th century, the most visionary educators foresaw special demands being placed on education by the rapidly evolving economic and social conditions. The shift from an agricultural to an industrial way of life was changing not only how people organized their work, their families and their lives, but also how they responded to schooling and education — how they learned.

The changes in society and the changes in the nature of work placed new demands on education. For this reason, the early 20th century was a period of tremendous innovation and experimentation with new educational philosophies and approaches. Educational institutions changed, the focus of curriculum changed, and teaching methods and philosophies changed. Classrooms were run according to very rigid rules of conduct. Behavior became as important as demonstration of knowledge, and failures at either of these tasks might well bring about the application of the "hick'ry stick." Punishment and reward became standards of operation in 20th century classrooms.

The progressive education movement was the industrial society's answer to the new needs in education. The progressives, of whom John Dewey is one of the most well known thinkers, began to develop curricula that were far more encompassing than the basic three Rs. Progressive education was pluralistic, and it included industrial training, agricultural education and social education. Dewey even proposed that the educational system should take on the job of socialization of immigrant populations. In 1901, Dewey wrote *The Child and the Curriculum,* the first of several books in which he espoused the idea of teaching by doing rather than rote memorization in the classroom. He called for a curriculum that combined liberal and vocational education, and which enlarged personal experiences "by furnishing their context, background and outlook" to the present community life (Dewey, 1916). Although he did not think in terms of "generational learning styles," the concept of enlarging personal experience by considering "context, background, and outlook" is certainly consistent with this thinking. The thrust was to provide appropriate education for young people relevant to the work they would be doing after they finished their schooling, and the theory was that if their education drew from their past experiences and addressed their futures, it would be of greater value and interest to the learners.

An important part of Dewey's philosophy was that children learn best when they are able to relate their learning to an area of personal interest or value. Progressive education was very learner centered, and recognized individual differences in how students learn. One aspect of Dewey's application of the progressive education theory was to incorporate social collaboration and group learning into the classroom. These approaches have some currency today, and classrooms might function quite differently than they do if subsequent reformers had not enhanced Dewey's ideas to make them more functional in an industrial economy.

One of the best known educational reform plans which grew out of the progressive movement, the Gary Plan, was developed in Gary, Indiana between 1908 and 1915 by school superintendent, William Wirt. (Cohen, 2002). Wirt adopted Dewey's educational philosophy and implemented a system of education unlike anything ever tried before — a system which ultimately led to a pedagogy that reflected the needs of leaders in industry and of employers in the nation's factories and mills. Leaders in industry looked to public education to help socialize workers during a period when there was a great deal of unrest in the labor force.

> "The argument is made that the reason there are labor riots and strikes is because the family can't manage their [sic] budget," explains Joel Spring, historian. "So home economics becomes a big issue. If the woman learns how to cook and the worker goes to work well fed and works hard, and knows that there will be a good meal when he returns home, he doesn't stop at the saloon and he comes directly home. And we will have industrial peace through home economics. So the school was suddenly the panacea for everything that was going on in society." (PBS Film Series, 2001).

This was a heavy charge to lay at the feet of American educators, but it was a charge that was embraced and which remains, implicitly, a central part of the mission of American public schools. The Gary plan, which was adopted by hundreds of school systems throughout the country, incorporated ways to run schools more efficiently, provided for more practical work, and developed ways to coordinate specific levels of work. The school facilities were divided into areas of specific function, such as playground, classroom, laboratory, auditorium, and shop areas. Schools were open six days a week, and two schools ran simultaneously in the same building to assure that the facility was constantly utilized to the maximum degree possible.

Other educational plans such as the Dalton Plan (1919) divided academic work into contract units, which students worked to complete in a specified amount of time. Increasingly, by the end of the second decade of the 20th century, the schools had begun to operate more and more like the factories that would benefit from the graduates of public education. Wirt himself referred to high-school diplomas as work certificates. It was clear that public school education had become, for the majority, about becoming trained, "certified" and socialized to work in the nation's factories. (Cohen, 2002). As the concepts of progressive education took hold, schools began to develop a curriculum that was based on the idea that, by having everyone together in the same place, schools could offer a "standardized 'conveyer belt' curriculum" (Jensen, 1998a) that would serve everyone equally. This model drew from business, religion and sociology. It emphasized useful skills like obedience, orderliness, unity and respect for authority. To be successful in the world of work, it was important to respect authority, be on time, follow rules, keep to schedules, and follow directions. One of the great contradictions of progressive education was that, while it embraced the philosophy of the importance of the learner experience and encouraged a consideration of the uniqueness of the individual, it led to the institutionalization of processes in a paradigm that had very little tolerance for individual differences, and which became very teacher-centered. Schools increasingly mirrored the factory environments into which their students would most often graduate.

The idea flourished that punishment and reward would improve student behavior, and by extension, learning. Indeed, one of the key goals of education in the early industrial era was to socialize the behavior of the immigrants who worked or would be working in American factories, so behavior became a key focus of the educational experience. In the pedagogy of the 20th century, educators increasingly adopted the idea that rewards and punishment were the best ways to reinforce desired behaviors or to extinguish undesirable ones. There was little or no awareness that external rewards have no effect or even negative effect on the ability of learners to complete complex cognitive tasks (Jensen, 1998). Educational philosophy hurtled forward, incorporating a system of punishments (the "hick'ry" stick in the first half of the 20th century, and detentions, withdrawal of reward, lowering of grades, and verbal criticism in the second half) that was well known and often despised by students. Rewards were less well defined, and often took the form of the "absence of punishment." Thus the stage was set for the shift of focus in public schools from rewarding academic achievement to punishing undesirable behavior and rewarding good behavior.

There are many parallels between the changing forces in society that prescient educators recognized one hundred years ago, and those of today. In the early 1900s, society was changing from an agricultural base to an industrial base. In the 21st century, society is moving from an industrial to an information or technological base. The needs and demands for success in the new world of the 21st century have tremendous implications for education.

In addition to the current shifts that will cause us all to restructure how we live, learn and recreate, there is another challenge for educators in today's world. In today's classrooms and in today's workplaces, there are adults spanning four generations. The oldest workers are in their 70s and even 80s. The youngest are in their teens. It is entirely possible in today's workplace and classroom to have someone's great-grandmother sitting beside someone who is not yet 20 years old. Never before has this kind of age diversity been present in our classrooms, and never before have teachers had to face the challenge of successfully teaching adults with such a wide range of outlook, experience and context.

In order for teachers to respond to this amazing diversity, it is critically important for them to understand how context, outlook and background impact learning. John Dewey saw these factors as key to effective education a hundred years ago, and they are even more critical in today's vastly more diverse world.

Some educational philosophers believe that by the 1960s, the progressive education movement had collapsed, but careful observation will reveal that many of the educational approaches, beliefs and attitudes of the early 20th century pedagogy, which were designed to socialize a population of factory workers for a manufacturing economy, are as present in today's classrooms as they were in 1920. In subsequent chapters, we will explore how the educational philosophies of the last century persist in our thinking, and how they affect our success in the 21st century classroom.

While the world is changing at a pace with which it is almost impossible for us to keep up, our schools are, in the main, still deeply rooted in the pedagogy and structures of the last century. Our schools are still socializing students to be successful in a manufacturing and industrial economy, even though U.S. industry is waning as manufacturers seek lower labor and operation costs in other countries, and technology and information workers are replacing manufacturing and factory workers. The nature of work for today's young adults will be very different from the work they may have taken on a hundred years ago, but our structures are still preparing them - or trying to prepare them - to be good factory workers. The different nature of work in the 21st century speaks to a need for a different kind of educational experience - one that will equip students to take their place in a very different economy than the one their parents knew.

As the industrial age spawned educational structures that, in some ways at least, were right for the new demands of an industrial economy, today's educators are challenged to build an educational experience that is right for the needs of the information age and the age of technology. The new work that will run the United States, and increasingly the global economy, is work that schools are not preparing students to take on. The new skill sets that tomorrow's workers will need are poorly addressed in many of today's classrooms. At a time when the information glut of our era demands increasing critical thinking and analysis skills, we find our system geared toward standardized testing and assessment. Many educators believe this actually reduces skills of critical and analytical evaluation as a result of "teaching to the test" and over-emphasis of areas to be tested at the expense of other learning (Ontario Secondary School Teachers Federation, 2001).

There is a steady movement in schools toward using more technology. Too often, however, the potential of technology is lost because it is used within an outdated and dysfunctional educational paradigm. As yet, there has been no fundamental philosophical shift to prepare students for the world they will inhabit and work in as adults, and there is no general acknowledgement that the strategies of the last century may be woefully inadequate for the present one.

Chapter 4: Learning and the Brain

I could while away the hours
Conferrin' with the flowers
Consultin' with the rain
And my head, I'd be scratchin'
While my thoughts were busy hatchin'
If I only had a brain.
I'd unravel ev'ry riddle
For any individ'le
In trouble or in pain
With the thoughts you'd be thinkin'
You could be another Lincoln,
If you only had a brain...

Source: The Wizard of Oz

In 1900, when Frank L. Baum wrote the *Wizard of Oz,* society was experiencing a shift not unlike what we are experiencing today. The shift then, as we have noted, was from the agricultural to the industrial age. We are now moving from the industrial to the information age. In *The Wonderful World of Oz,* described by Henry M. Littlefield as a parable on populism, the naïve (albeit wise) scarecrow has his parallel in the American farmer, who, since the turn of the last century, has been increasingly characterized as brainless and simple (Parker, 1994).

The shift from the societal values of the farm to the factory brought with it a changing perception of the importance of "intelligence." Whereas it was not necessary to know how to read in order to be a successful farmer, for example, one needed to have basic literacy skills to succeed in the new work environment of the industrial era. In order to learn from books, one had to be "smart." During the early years of the 20th century, more young people entered school and remained there than at any previous period in history. By 1918, every state in America had a compulsory attendance law, requiring young people to attend school. Being "smart" was equivalent to being successful (America at School: 1894-1915). The advent of compulsory education brought more changes to the educational setting. Until 1918, an unhappy student could simply choose to leave school. After that time, students had to attend school whether they wanted to or not. This led to an even greater emphasis on behavior, as the numbers of students in classrooms grew and teachers had to manage more students in their classes while maintaining order and discipline.

Partly as a result of the Progressive movement, there was, during this time, a substantial growth in the belief that individuals were competent to do certain types of work based on the measure of their IQ. IQ tests became increasingly popular in the early years of the 20th century. During these years and until the late 1950s, schools "tracked" students based on their test scores. During this period as well, it was popularly held that immigrants, minorities, and the poor were less intelligent than the white, male upper and middle classes, and the IQ tests, which were biased toward the latter group, seemed to support that theory. The IQ tests were used as a means to filter students into occupations that were "suitable" for their abilities (Mondale, 2002).

The brain, it was clear to educators of the time, was the center of intelligence, and therefore, it was (and to some extent still is) believed that some people were born with brains that equipped them to be academically successful, and that others were not — and there were tests that could identify each group. By this time, there seemed to be less commitment to the idea that there might be ways to teach that would address differences in how people learn, or that some people might learn differently from others.

We know a great deal more today about the brain and how it functions than we did even ten years ago, and we know vastly more than we did 50 years ago. We now know that behavior often tells us very little about what is actually going on in the brain. Through the use of technology, we are able to see differences in brain structure, and to measure the production of neural activity and chemical production in the brain that affect how we behave and more importantly, how we learn.

In *The Wizard of Oz*, Baum's scarecrow, cowardly lion and tin man represented three different human traits — intelligence, confidence and emotion/compassion — as each character, respectively, sought a brain, courage, and a heart. These attributes have long been thought of as separate and unrelated aspects of being. In fact, there has been much debate in science, literature and philosophy, about the dichotomy of reason and emotion. In *Descartes' Error*, Antonio Demasio (1995) a noted neurobiologist, explores the inextricable links between reason and emotion, and builds a powerful case that reason is dependent upon and inseparable from emotion. Rather than describing the mind as separate from the body, Demasio describes it as one single, interactive biological system that works in concert to assure survival.

It is essential that educators understand the link between reason and emotion in order to develop a pedagogy that serves learners' needs in the 21st century. Emotion is very important to the education process because it drives attention, which drives learning and memory. Emotion, which occurs unconsciously in response to a myriad of environmental experiences both within and outside of the classroom and in response to both conscious and unconscious memory, often leads to behaviors that, to teachers at least, seem inappropriate. Our brain, being cautious, believes that over-reaction to perceived threats (which trigger some emotions) is better than under-reaction. And our brains don't chemically distinguish between the threat of a hungry lion poised to pounce and a student's fear of failure in presenting a book report, or between an unexpected loud sound, or an internalized memory triggered by a sound, comment or event within the classroom. The fear that is experienced triggers production of the same brain chemicals, regardless of source. Thus, misbehavior is often perceived when a student is actually reacting to internal, emotional stimuli. When stress occurs, attention to anything other than the stressor diminishes, further exacerbating the problem and reducing the effectiveness of learning.

In addition to the link that Demasio suggests between reason and emotion, he, as well as others, describes the brain as being "an adaptive organ." A critical function of the brain, he says, is to respond rapidly to the environment and to equip the organism with the best responses for survival within the environment it inhabits. The brain, he says, interacts not only with the external environment, but also with the internal processes of the body and the brain itself. Behavior is intimately linked to what is happening in both the internal and the external environments. The brain takes its cues from a myriad of hormones, body chemicals and internal electrical signals that have been developed within each individual organism over time, in response to the unique environment the organism inhabits.

> To a first approximation, the overall function of the brain is to be well informed about what goes on in the rest of the body, the body proper; about what goes on in itself; and about the environment surrounding the organism, so that suitable, survivable accommodations can be achieved between the organism and environment (p 90).

A second point that Demasio emphasizes is that our reason is not separate from our biology. Mind is part and parcel of our biological being. This is a key issue for educators, who must consider that how human beings, including students, react in certain situations is strongly influenced by the inextricable link between mind and body, and the communication that is seamless between the brain and other biological systems.

> Consider what happens when we move away briskly to avoid a falling object. There is a situation which calls for prompt action (e.g., falling object; there are options for action (to duck or not) and each has a different consequence. However, in order to select the response, we use neither conscious (explicit) knowledge nor a conscious reasoning strategy. The requisite knowledge was once conscious, when we first learned that falling objects may hurt us and that avoiding them... is better than being hit. But experience with such scenarios as we grew up made our brains solidly pair the provoking stimulus with the most advantageous response. The "strategy" for response selection now consists of activating the strong link between stimulus and response, such that the implementation

of the response comes *automatically* and *rapidly*, although one can willfully try to preempt it (pp . 166-167).

There are at least three conclusions that educators can draw from Demasio's assertions. One is that each individual possesses a unique brain, because no individual inhabits an environment that is identical in every way, both internally and externally, to that of any other individual. While we might accept that some of these differences are quite small, and that we can have understanding overall about how the brain works, we might also agree that there will be some differences based on the unique experiences of individuals.

The second conclusion, which might be arrived at by extension of Demasio's ideas, is that as environment changes — altered as it is by changes in culture, demography, technology, and other societal changes - then individuals adapt to those changes and have ways of thinking, feeling and learning that may be different from those of individuals in generations preceding or following to a degree that is greater than the differences among individuals within the same societal cohort.

The third is that the link between mind and body, reason and emotion, is so powerful and not under conscious control, that events and situations which occur during the learning process may have significantly different and profound impacts on behavior, perception and learning. Viewed in terms of Frank L. Baum's symbolism in *The Wizard of Oz,* the heart, the brain and the will are not three separate entities, but rather one system of interdependent relationships that are all essential to how an individual thinks, behaves and learns.

In the middle of the last century, educational theorists were influenced by the work of behaviorists such as B. F. Skinner and John Watson, whose ideas were essentially that, while we don't know a lot about what is going on inside the brain, we can see the behaviors that result from the brain's activity. Therefore, the thinking went, we should be able to measure behaviors and change them by rewarding those behaviors we want and punishing those behaviors we don't want (Jensen, 1998). Many current educators still operate within this paradigm or some slight variation of it.

The idea of rewarding desired behaviors and punishing negative behaviors seems at first blush to have a great deal of merit. However, neuroscientist Eric Jensen (1998) asserts that in an educational setting, such an approach may be of minimal value or may even be a negative factor in learning. Deci, Valleran, Pelletier and Ryan, 1991 and Kohn, 1993 (as cited in Jensen, 1998, assert that

> The stimulus-response rewards popularized by behaviorism were effective only for simple physical actions. But schools often try to reward students for solving challenging cognitive problems, writing creatively, and designing and completing projects. There's an enormous difference in how the human brain responds to rewards for simple and complex problem-solving tasks. Short-term rewards can temporarily stimulate simple physical responses, but more complex behaviors are usually impaired, not helped by rewards (p 63).

In *The Wizard of Oz,* the scarecrow was asked by the blackbird, "What the thunder would you do with common sense?" The Scarecrow replied, "Would be pleasin' just to reason out the reason of the whiches and the whyness and the whence" (Dreams Do Come True, 1998). Subsequent research has added credibility to the scarecrow's observation. The activity of thinking, learning, and achieving brings intrinsic rewards.

The assumption of the behaviorists, that learning is primarily dependent upon external reward, is flawed. The brain has its own means for rewarding learning, and it is much more effective than any external reward. Rats, and humans (and scarecrows) as well, have a strong impetus to seek novelty and new experiences with no obvious potential for reward. It is possible that novelty seeking may be a survival strategy, in that it could lead to new sources of food, shelter or safety, but it has been found to be a strong drive in laboratory rats. Studies confirm that curiosity — the mere pursuit of information — has intrinsic value (Jensen, 1998).

Jensen also notes that the brain makes its own rewards — chemicals that create a pleasant feeling. The brain produces natural opiates, which can produce a natural high similar to that of morphine, alcohol, nicotine, heroin or cocaine in response to behaviors that are pleasant, such as affection, sex, caring or achievement. Thus, the brain rewards cerebral learning with good feelings, and this is a far more powerful motivator for learning than any external reward.

Reward comprises half of the arsenal of weapons for those educators who employ behaviorist strategies in their classrooms, and punishment comprises the other half. If rewards are used to encourage desired behaviors, then punishment is the obvious tool to address negative behaviors. In the early part of the 20th century, corporal punishment was the norm. In *Child Labor,* Julia Johnsen (1925) notes that out of some 800 children questioned, 269 gave as their one reason for preferring work in the factory to school, that they were not hit there.

> Children fear and dread corporal punishment. Inspecting the stock yards one day, I literally stumbled over a little creature who, on being brought to the surface and into the light of the office, proved to be not yet fourteen. Upon being told he was not old enough to work and must go to school, he took his pay envelope and crawled behind a large pile of dusty wrapping-paper and boards in the corner of the room. When we had removed his barrier, piece by piece, in order to reach him, we found him pressed against the wall, weeping miserably.
> As I walked home with him, I asked him:
> "Don't you like to go to school?"
> "No," he answered. "I want my job," and began weeping afresh.
> "What," I said in despair, remembering the dark, damp basement in which I had found him, "What is it you like so much about your job?"
> "The boss" he answered, "don't never hit me."
> "Did they hit you at school?"
> "Yes."
> "What for?"
> "They hits ye if ye don't learn, and they hits ye if ye whisper, and they hits ye if ye have string in yer pocket, and they hits ye if yer seat squeaks, and they hits ye if ye scrape yer feet, and they hits ye if ye don't stan' up in time, and they hits ye if yer late, and they hits ye if ye ferget the page" (pp 144-145).

Twenty-first century educators may read these words with dismay, and may feel relief that such an environment does not exist in public schools today. If so, that relief is misplaced, since there is ample evidence that, although the form of punishment has changed to a great degree, many schools are still enamored of the notion that managing student behavior is the first mission of the education system, and that without firm discipline, chaos would reign.

Writing in The Journal of School Psychology (1998), Hyman and Perone note that the emphasis on stemming student aggression and misbehavior may have led to an insidious negative feedback structure where the very problems that schools seek to remedy are exacerbated by the techniques for managing them. Student aggression against peers, school staff, and property is a popular topic in the media and a great concern of the public. However, analysis of crime statistics suggests the problem of school violence is vastly overstated. This results in reliance on inappropriate or inadequate policies aimed at prevention and remediation of problems. Further, there is a side of school violence that receives relatively little attention. Victimization of students by teachers, administrators, and other school staff, most often in the name of discipline, is seldom recognized for its potential to contribute to student misbehavior, alienation, and aggression. Included in this type of victimization are recently introduced intrusive and sometimes abusive law enforcement procedures, such as strip searches and the use of undercover agents; historically accepted or tolerated disciplinary procedures such as corporal punishment, still allowed in 23 states; and teachers' verbalizations that constitute psychological maltreatment. How these practices may contribute to school violence is documented in survey data, anecdotal evidence, and clinical studies. School psychologists should become more involved in prevention programs and in the implementation of a suggested research agenda.

The importance of recognizing the impact of perceived threat, in the form of punishment in our schools, cannot be overstated. Although corporal punishment is less common today than it was a century ago, it is still permitted in almost half of states. The forms of discipline that are most common, including demerits, detention, loss of privileges, lowering of grades, verbal criticism and embarrassment in front of peers, and suspension can be as damaging to effective learning as corporal punishment.

Jensen (1998) notes that such disciplinary strategies are often unsuccessful, and provides compelling evidence, based on brain biology, that the culture in which such management behaviors predominate may produce an environment that, even if it does not lead to violence is, at best, very ill-suited for learning. Further, Jensen notes, significant stress or violence in early childhood can actually rewire the brain, diminishing the effectiveness of the built-in reward system within the brain. These children have learned to thrive just by surviving, and the disciplinary strategies used by most teachers will fall short. For other children, the disciplinary strategies may stimulate fear or anxiety and lead to reductions in academic performance.

It is well documented that emotionally stressful school environments can reduce a student's ability to learn, and can have a negative impact on academic performance (Sylwester, 1995). Even mild stress can have noticeable impact. In a world as complex and multi-faceted as the one in which we live, stress is a constant in the lives of both children and adults. It is important to recognize that the multiple stresses of just living in the 21st century, especially when they are exacerbated by the punitive culture of many schools, may lead to undesirable behaviors, reduced motivation and lowered academic performance.

Why can't students today sit still and listen?

Many have observed that today's students are different from students in the past. They are less motivated, more restless, demand entertainment in the classroom, are less prepared to learn, unable to focus, and otherwise decidedly inferior to the sterling student of yesteryear. The impact of television, computers, the Internet and video games upon student behavior and performance has been endlessly debated. Some have suggested that what they perceive as increased prevalence of low motivation and lack of attentiveness can be traced to the negative influences of electronic media including TV, video games and computers. Such assumptions fail to consider the cross-cultural implications of these conclusions. In Japan, for example, a country even more "wired" than our own, where video games and other forms of technological innovation originate, students are ten times less likely to be identified as having attention deficit issues than are students in the United States (TePas, 1996 & Wichman, 2000).

Parents and frustrated educators point to the rise in the number of students diagnosed with ADD/ADHD, or that students are unmotivated and inattentive. Others assert that there is too great a tendency in the United

States to label behavior as problematic that would be considered normal at other times in history. Today's children spend a great deal of time in structured activity - more than half their discretionary time (Hoforth & Sandburg, 2001). This creates some conflicts in the settings that children occupy for most of their day, (next to sleep, children spend more time in school each week than in any other activity), since there is a strong focus on learning in the formal educational setting, using techniques that require sitting and attending to information as it is being presented.

The human brain, as we have previously seen, is designed to seek novelty, to explore the environment, and to reward this behavior when learning occurs. This, says Robert Sylwester (1995b), in *A Celebration of Neurons: An Educator's Guide to the Human Brain*, creates a "curricular dilemma."

> The design of our brain's attentional system... evolved to quickly recognize and respond to sudden dramatic changes that signal physical predatory danger, and to ignore or merely monitor the steady states, subtle differences and gradual changes that don't carry a sense of immediate alarm. (pp 78-84).

Previously we learned that a key function of the brain is to adapt to the environment and to optimize an organism's likelihood of survival. To do this in nature, the brain has to hyper-focus, i.e., attend to many different stimuli within the environment.

Think of a wild bunny munching on tender shoots of grass in an open meadow. It would be folly for the bunny to focus only on the grass. It must also attend to the scents, sights, smells, and sounds around it in order to avoid becoming dinner for a hungry fox or hawk. Human brains are also focusing on many different activities in the external environment. To demand in the classroom that the brain limit its focus to just one activity, particularly one that the brain does not interpret as "novel" such as learning an algebra problem is doomed to failure.

> While our attentional system has a built-in bias for high contrast, novelty, and emotional overtones, the curriculum presents a predictable universe: C-A-T always spells *cat*, and 6 times 5 always equals 30. We want students to solve such problems automatically and unemotionally — to achieve mastery — but mastery reduces students' need to actively attend to a

process. It's a dilemma: the effective teaching of skills can reduce students' active attention to the process. Moreover, routine, low-contrast curricular tends to bore students who spend hours with video games and TV programs... high contrast behaviors that attract active attention. (Sylwester 1995c).

Add to this that the brain functions in normal 90-minute cyclical fluctuations, and that the brain needs "processing time" or "play time" when engaged in intense or complex cognitive activities. Attention fluctuates based on normal brain activity cycles. Although people vary in their cycles, most experience a sharp rise in their attentional capability around 6 a. m., which causes us to wake up, and maintain relatively high levels during the morning. Attention declines during the afternoon. (Sylwester, 1995d). Some high schools have scheduled classes so that those demanding the most attention and covering the most challenging topics are offered during morning hours when attentional skills are at their peak.

Jensen (1998) notes "genuine, external attention can be sustained at a high an constant level for only a short time, generally about 10 minutes or less." This, he says, is a biological function possibly related to survival. In the classroom, demanding constant attention is counterproductive.

Workers need 5 to 10 minute breaks every hour and a half. Why would students or staff be any different? That would fit right into the "bottom" of the 90-110 minute cycle... Much of what we learn cannot be processed consciously; it happens too fast. We need time to process it. Second, in order to create new meaning, we need internal time. Meaning is always generated from within, not externally. Third, after each new learning experience, we need time for the learning to imprint... In order to proceed or "figure it all out," a student must "go internal" and give up that "external" attention. As educators, we must allow for this creative time if we want new learning to occur (pp 45-46).

If we consider the brain's biological design, it is possible for us to draw some important conclusions about education. First, inattentiveness and activity are not always signs of lack of interest or motivation. Second, by incorporating appropriate strategies into our teaching, we can allow for the "natural inattention" that occurs in the learning process and increase the students' effectiveness in learning new material. We will explore this idea further in subsequent chapters, particularly as it relates to gender-based differences in classroom behavior.

It has become abundantly clear that there are structural differences in the brains of people who have been diagnosed with ADD/ADHD. One must wonder whether the epidemic of neurological dysfunction in some measure results from the misidentification of normally active young people whose brains are telling them that they need to move, to explore, and to seek novelty. Psychologists have noted that there are more than 50 disorders that can mimic ADD/ADHD, including anxiety, and that some behavior that is considered to be "hyperactive" or "inattentive" may be quite developmentally appropriate and "normal." Our brains are not optimized for sitting for 7.5 hours a day in classrooms and seeking mastery of activities that soon become routine (not novel).

It seems clear that schools are ill-prepared to respond to the individual learning needs and styles of today's students, and that in far too many schools, there is a decided lack of sensitivity to any student who can't sit still and focus on the learning task at hand. At the root of much of the teaching that goes on today is the notion, dating back 100 years, that students need to sit quietly, focus on their work, and not fidget, wiggle or become distracted. So serious is the transgression of lack of attention that in 1902, the collection of behaviors that we now label ADD/ADHD was described by Dr. George Still in the British journal, Lancet, as chronic "morbid defects in moral control" (Martin, 2002). It is an interesting coincidence that the identification of these "defects in moral control" was first described at the beginning of the industrial age, and the behaviors have persisted and increased in the population under a variety of names (restlessness disorder, minimal brain damage disorder, etc.).

To further complicate the problem of attentiveness, students in today's classrooms are still expected to function in settings designed to educate them for work in a world that no longer exists. They live in the 21st century and learn in the 19th century. Such dissonance surely creates stress, particularly when the structure of rewards and punishments is employed to encourage student to conform behaviorally to the expectations of the factory model. Further, failure to conform behaviorally results in additional stress, and thus we find students "unmotivated," "inattentive" and lacking initiative. Today's generation of learners is quite different from past generations of learners in some key ways, primarily because the world is quite different. The values, expectations, behaviors and motivators for the 21st century are very different, if not substantively at least in form, from those of the past.

Teachers frequently mention the lack of motivation, the desire on the part of students to be entertained, and the difficulties in getting students to "take responsibility" for their own learning. This book will address the issues related to how today's young people learn best, and will explore strategies and approaches that can be put into practice in any classroom, that can make a difference for today's students. It is essential, however, for teachers to accept that the brain, in addition to learning in the classroom, is concurrently engaged in a myriad of other activities: managing stress, optimizing survival, handling complex emotions, processing cognitive information, and being vigilant for threats and danger. There are practical steps that teachers can use to help students toward academic success while respecting that the brain is incapable of being focused solely on what is being taught in the classroom.

Chapter 5: Culture and Community in a Changing Society

...There are no precedents to guide us,
no wisdom that wasn't made for a simpler age.
We have changed our environment more quickly
than we know how to change ourselves.
— Walter Lippmann, 1914

Social change has been part of human community since the earliest days of history. Human beings have always organized into social groups as one way to insure survival, and these social groups have always been organic and changing. Shifts in power hierarchies, degree of personal autonomy, control of economic resources, access to information, and influence of diverse segments of society have always fluctuated in response to changes in the social environment. In general, these fluctuations have been driven by changes in technology, availability of economic resources, demands for changes in access to wealth and autonomy within a society, demographic shifts and other changes in the structure of national and global communities.

The evolution of community cultures is not linear, but rather tends to progress in a wave-like fashion. During the early years of the 20th century, advances in technology and information, changes in the structure of the economy and an influx of immigrants were all part of the mix in the

41

United States as the nation evolved from an agricultural to an urban-industrial society. The pace of change was equivalent to that of the current time, and had an equally profound impact on the daily lives of citizens. The rapid social, economic and technological changes outpaced the speed of change in culture, attitudes, and beliefs of the population, and it played havoc with the existing structure of community life and with the relationships, networks, and support systems that had characterized the small, agricultural towns of the time.

The advent of the railroad and the telegraph, telephones and electricity provided what, in those times was an unimaginable explosion in the ability to communicate, to travel from one place to another, and in the amount of information available to the average person. It was an age of information as well as of industry. The changes in technology also changed the nature of work, education and leisure, just as we see in today's world with the impact of digital technology on society.

There emerged new classes of workers - the "white collar" workers (administrators, executives, managers) and low-skill, low-wage workers. The gaps between the income of skilled and unskilled workers were substantial, as they are today. Not only did the nature of work change, but also the *scale* of enterprise was revolutionized by technology. Robert Putnam (2000) writes that in 1865, the typical New England mill employed 200 to 300 people. Business became dominated by large corporations, which grew in size as well as number. The number of factories in America quadrupled between 1865 and 1900. In 1915, the first Ford Motor plant employed at least 15,000 workers. The political effects of these changes echo those of today. Historian Stephen Diner (as cited in Putnam, 2000) notes that:

> Middle class Americans... watched as the trusts manipulated members of Congress and used the courts and federal power to suppress dissent from farmers and workers. Government, which according to American ideals should represent the will of the people, appeared a captive of special interests. (p. 374)

There was much debate about the value of the new communication technologies of the time. Some, including William Allen White, (as cited in Putnam, 2000), argued that it would enable the conversion of a vast nation into a:

...neighborhood... The electric wire, the iron pipe, the street railroad, the daily newspaper, the telephone... have made us all one body... There are no outlanders. It is possible for all men to understand one another... (p. 376)

Others, less certain about the universal beneficence of technology in communication, were concerned about how to integrate the new ways of communication with face-to-face exchange. John Dewey and Mary Parker Follett (as cited in Putnam, 2000) were concerned about the impact of technology on community life. These concerns echo the present-day debate about the Internet.

As in contemporary times, gender roles began to change. Dewey observed with dismay that:

The invasion of the community by the new and relatively impersonal and mechanical modes of combined human behavior is the outstanding fact of modern life... The machine age, in developing the Great Society, has invaded and partially disintegrated the small communities of former times without generating a Great Community. (p. 377)

Mary Parker Follett asserted that:

Real solidarity will never be accomplished except by beginning somewhere the joining of one small group with another. Only by actual union, not by imagination... can varied... groups be made part of a sound, normal urban life (p. 377).

Not only was technology changing the way people received information and communicated with each other, it changed patterns of leisure. As technology today has made available video games, television, interactive Internet, DVDs, CDs, and portable players for all of the above — and other diversions unheard of just a few decades ago — so it did at the turn of the last century as well. The inventions of the phonograph and movies made a new kind of low-cost entertainment widely available.

New storefront theaters, dubbed *nickelodeons*, were a wildly successful innovation. Appearing first in 1905, nickelodeons featured movie shows all day long, and in contrast to the vaudeville theaters, which had showed many actuality films, the nickelodeons featured more fictional films. The first nickelodeon was built in Pittsburgh in June 1905 by Harry Davis, a vaudeville magnate. Soon nickelodeons began to appear in cities around the country.

In her book, *The Transformation of Cinema,* Eileen Bowser (1994) writes that by 1908, there were approximately 8,000 nickelodeons in the United States. They attracted a wide audience, including women and children, and their frequent showings made it possible for almost anyone to find the time to view a show.

Other changes were afoot in the beginning of the 20th century as well. Gender roles began to be less distinct. The Gibson Girl and the "It" Girl represented the new personae of women in society. More women began to pursue higher education. Women gained the right to vote. Society had been turned upside down in every sector, and there was a widespread sense that the social bonds of community had been severed. Many believed that "in the newer social order. . .relations tended to be superficial, the restraints imposed by public opinion weak, and common cause with one's neighbor lacking" (Putnam, 2000). Meredith Wilson, born in 1902, wrote the musical, *The Music Man,* in the middle of the 20th century. Set in small-town America in 1912, this production was an enduring hit. It embodies many of the popular attitudes of that earlier period and derives its humor from the contrast between the conflicting values of the 19th and 20th centuries.

In our own times, there is a sense that community life is fractured and that relations are superficial. Writing in *The Shelter of Each Other* 1996), psychotherapist Mary Pipher describes a culture that is "at war with families." Today, she says, we lack the support of extended families and communities that were commonplace in simpler times, 50 to 100 years ago. Unlike the small, close-knit communities of yesteryear, in today's world we no longer have "primary relationships with people" in which we know things about them - like where they go to church, whether they have a dog or not, and what kinds of books they read. We know people, she says, through their roles—as the pharmacist, the doctor, the clerk at the super market. These relationships are superficial, and rob us of the support and nurture that true community provides. Pipher (1998), in an interview for *Educational Leadership,* describes some of the changes that affect children and families and notes, "We're starting to have a culture in which adults are afraid of children and children are afraid of adults." Just as in 1912, we have 'trouble in River City.'

It is interesting that our own age is currently washed with a wave of nostalgia for a simpler time in the past. In non-credit enrichment programs, we see a preponderance of classes focusing on topics that indicate a wish to retreat into a period of time where life was less complex. From "Antique Collecting" to "Tours of Historic Bed and Breakfast Inns," people are repairing to the past in search of some respite from the sometimes-overwhelming pace at which society is hurtling into unknown areas. In our thinking, that simpler time is those years in the early part of our century when society was also awash in nostalgia for a simpler time. Indeed, "nostalgia" was officially declared a mental illness by the U.S. Military in 1918 and was so classified as late as 1942. It was a category that was created during the war for soldiers who had an inordinate attachment to their motherland, the home they left behind. So nostalgia was classified as a form of mental depravity or derangement.

The past that "never was" was part of the discussion of a panel at MIT in November, 1998. Participants suggest that selective recollection of the past renders us nostalgic for a reality that never existed. Further, Alexander Jablokov, one of the panelists notes, "It's amazing how often revolutions disguise themselves as cultural revivals. You can go back to pick and choose from whatever you had in the past that you enjoyed, and truly transform your society into a state in which it never existed before. It has always been a tradition to claim that it's for traditional reasons that you are doing it." The panel noted that it is possible to mythologize the past, to identify one aspect for which pleasant associations exist, and project that reality upon the whole of an earlier time (WGBH Radio).

Today, when we lament the loss of community, the degradation of our cities, the stresses on our young people and the inequities of our governing bodies, we long for the days when a deal could be sealed with a handshake, when children were innocent and compliant, when neighbors shoveled your walk when you were sick, and when we didn't have to lock our doors at night. The good ol' days - for which we generally advocate a return - because then, people had the right values, and everything was in good order.

We do not long, however, for child labor, sweatshops, political corruption, violence and war, urban blight, out-of-control-crime and homelessness. These societal afflictions, or versions of them, existed as much at the turn of the 19th century as they do today. Now, as in the good ol' days, our society was faced with massive change and uncertainty, and people had before them, as we do, the formidable task of shaping a society that could function optimally within a world that had changed, seemingly overnight, from one reality to another (WGBH Radio).

The social turmoil at the turn of the last century gave birth to one of the most vital and creative periods in the history of the United States. The Progressive Era, as it was called, saw unprecedented innovation in education, reform of social programs, governmental structures and political philosophy. Creative thinkers fashioned new structures to facilitate the need for human interaction, social support, communication and networking — the infrastructure upon which all successful societies depend. Many of the new structures that emerged looked quite different from those of earlier times.

Trade and professional associations provided support and communication networks for communities of people with shared goals and interests. Educational innovations resulted in new ways of teaching and viewing learning that focused on the learner rather than the teacher. Child labor laws protected children from oppression at the hands of greedy industrialists. Philosophically the nation shifted from social Darwinism, a system in which the fittest would prevail and the weak would fall by the wayside, assuring the continuing progress of social evolution. Such a system, based on the "natural laws of the marketplace," and minimal governmental interference, ultimately gave way to a philosophy that society must be further democratized in order to assure every citizen the rights guaranteed by the Constitution. (Putnam, 2000).

There are signs that such reform is stirring the beginning of the 21st century as well. While nay-sayers decry the loss of "family values," the failure of the public school, and the loss of community, some of our youngest citizens are exhibiting a renewed social awareness and dedication to community and family. If change is to be engendered, if reform is to occur, and if the new technology and work of the 21st century is to be molded into a community structure that will serve the needs of society for the next 100 years, then the seeds of that change are already sprouting.

The two youngest generations in the United States today, generally referred to as Generation X and Generation Y, have already been characterized by some analysts as having "more traditional" values than those of the Baby Boom Generation. Zemke, Raines and Filipczak (2000), writing in *Generations at Work* notes that Generation Xers, those born roughly between 1965 and 1981, are strongly family oriented and strongly community/group oriented. This is a generation in search of family and community, having come of age without those nurturing relationships. Thus, these social relationships are highly sought after and highly valued.

The youngest generation, Generation Y (about 1981-present), is compared favorably to the WWII generation. In a recent study by Northwestern Mutual Life and the Harris organization of the attitudes and behaviors of 2,001 college students at 101 colleges, respondents felt the most affinity to their World War II-era grandparents and great-grandparents. They subscribe to a stricter moral code, care about manners, and believe in civic action (Zemke, Raines, and Filipczak, 1999). These generations are ones who will lead us into the new society of the 21st century, and already we can see the emergence of new ways of thinking that may usher in a second era of Progressive thought.

Chapter 6: Generations and Social Change

The children now love luxury. They have bad manners, contempt for authority; they show disrespect for adults, and love to talk rather than work or exercise. They no longer rise when adults enter the room. They contradict their parents, chatter in front of company, gobble down food at the table and intimidate their teachers.
—Socrates (469-399 B. C.)

There has probably never been a time when adults did not observe that the younger generation was, in nearly every way, less likely to succeed than their predecessors unless the youth experienced some miraculous turn-around in attitude and behavior. The staid perspective of adults has never been generous when evaluating the prospects of the younger elements in society. The question then becomes whether there are differences in generations that might account for disparities in outlook, perception, and behavior, or whether these dissimilarities are simply a result of the characteristic divergence in points of view that result from being in different stages of development and life-cycle.

In his groundbreaking book, *Bowling Alone,* Robert Putnam presents overwhelming evidence that there are significant, measurable differences in social attitudes and behavior that are unquestionably generational. By analyzing changes in attitude among similar age groups across a period of decades, Putnam (2000) has identified changes that clearly represent generational, not life-stage differences. Values have shifted significantly over the course of the last half-century. For example, in 1975, 38 percent of adults identified having "a lot of money" as an important element of "the good life." An equal number identified "having a job that contributes to the welfare of society" as an essential element as well. This survey was repeated every three years by the Roper organization, and by 1996, contributing to the welfare of society had dropped in importance to 32 percent, while those who felt it was important to have a lot of money had jumped to 63 percent. Having a second home, a second car, foreign travel, a job with above-average pay were values that rose significantly in the perception of requirements for "the good life." Other elements saw declines in importance, including a happy marriage, children, and an interesting job. The reasons for these changes, of course, are the result of generational values and replacement of less materialistic elders by a younger generation more concerned with material comfort (Putnam, 2000).

Differences in the generations are not confined to attitudes about material wealth. Putnam describes a transition from trust, civic engagement, cooperativeness, political involvement, participation in social and service organizations, church attendance and volunteerism which were characteristic of adults who were born before 1930, to lack of trust, withdrawal from involvement in civic and community life, "rampant individualism," (Putnam, 2000) privatization of entertainment and recreation, declines in volunteerism, declines in political activity such as voting, and reduced participation in social and service clubs, and in church attendance in generations born after World War II.

The subject of Putnam's analysis, the evolution of social and civic life in the United States over the past century, and of what he describes as a reduction in "social capital" is critical for educators to understand. Social capital, Putnam's term for those relationships, social ties, networks, and connections that bind us into a community, is in decline, and this in large measure, affects how generations view the world. The collection of shared values, attitudes and beliefs that guide our behavior as a society is no longer as universally embraced as it was 50 years ago. Putnam documents the gradual loosening of these ties since the middle of the century, and shows how, in each succeeding generation, the impact has been more apparent and has had more impact on daily life in America.

The Baby Boom generation (born 1946-1964) is quick to finger the generation that followed it, Generation X, (born 1965-1980) as a group of disengaged, cynical, and materialistic slackers with an overwhelming sense of entitlement. This generation, boomers point out, is observably devoid of the values that we have always held dear as a nation, and is, in the minds of many baby boomers and older adults, without much to redeem it. While Putnam documents that Generation X is, indeed, less engaged in civic life than the Baby Boom generation, and is more materialistic, less trusting, more cynical and less altruistic, he suggests that this generation represents the evolutionary outcome of a process that began with the Baby Boom, and which has continued unimpeded over the past 50 years. In reality, he notes that the oldest boomers are more likely to reflect the values of their predecessors and that, as attitudes are measured among younger adults, they are more likely to reflect that changes that are ascribed to Generation X (Putnam, 2000). In other words, Gen X is not a sudden aberration from the "normal" societal values. It simply reflects the culmination of change that has been evolving over the past five decades.

The changes that Putnam describes are attributable to many factors. From the Viet Nam War, which was the impetus for distrust of governments and institutions for Baby Boomers, to changes in family structure, the changes in global economy and the replacement of local enterprises with multinational corporations, pressures of time and money, sprawl, and the gradual loss of civic memory as our elders decline in number,[2] the changes in society over the past 50 years have been gradual but relentless (Putnam, 2000).

World War II, which in great measure shaped the values of the oldest adults in society, was a source of immeasurable unity of purpose, cooperativeness, striving toward a common goal, and national commitment - social capital. The values adopted during this time have diminished as the population has aged. In the middle of the century, another war affected another generation - as profoundly as the Second World War had affected their parents. The Viet Nam War, however, did not inspire a nation to unite in common purpose. It divided the nation along political and ideological lines. It was as divisive as the Second World War had been unifying. The debate and violence of the civil rights movement, the assassinations of John F. Kennedy and Martin Luther King, and the shame of Watergate were events that left the enormous cohort of Baby Boomers feeling tricked and betrayed. To an idealistic generation who cut their teeth on the patriotic and even nationalistic rhetoric of post-war America, the cognitive dissonance of the 60s was overwhelming. It created a generation increasingly distrusting of institutions, alienated from politics, and significantly less involved than their predecessors. Generation X is merely the logical outcome of that evolutionary process (Putnam, 2000).

Not only does Putnam document the changes in participation in key aspects of community life and in social attitudes, he also documents changes in school achievement linked to the degree of social capital within a state (Putnam, 2000). The extent to which states have a healthy social infrastructure is a predictor of school success and behavior for the children of that state. This phenomenon extends to individual communities, and conceivably to the culture within individual schools. One conclusion based on Putnam's research is that where there is common purpose, involvement, a sense of community, leadership, and resources for social and academic support within a school, there are also fewer behavior problems, a lower incidence of clinical depression among students, higher academic performance and higher scores on standardized tests. "Studies have found that student learning is influenced not only by what happens in school and at home, but also by social networks, norms, and trust in the school and in the wider community" (Putnam, 2000).

Society has changed remarkably over the past century. The changes have been profound at many different levels. The world we live in now is not the same world that our parents occupied, nor is it the same world our children know. It is a very different environment, and as we have seen, our experiences affect us not only as individuals but also as a culture. Because we will strive to act and interact within the structure of society as we perceive it, we can expect to see students whose behavior may be quite different from that of students even 20 years ago. There are different forces at play than there were in the past, and as adaptive beings, today's students will respond in the ways they perceive will give them greatest advantage within a very complex and rapidly changing society, just as those preceding them did. The catch is that each generation sees things a bit differently, and therefore may behave very differently within the learning environment.

Increasing understanding of the differences in how the generations view the world, and understanding the societal changes and cultural experiences that have given rise to these differences is one of the key purposes of this book. The second is to show how these differences in perception and experience affect motivation, behavior and attitudes about learning, and to suggest ways to structure the learning setting to meet the needs of different generations of learners. There are many considerations when designing curriculum and teaching strategies. In order to be optimally successful, generational biases and preferences that affect learning must be understood and respected.

Technology and Learning Style

There is, in today's classrooms and training rooms, a quiet revolution going on. There is a major paradigm shift that is being shaped by the communication tools of the 21st century, and this is impacting how students learn and how teachers must begin to teach. If we accept that learning preferences are, to some extent, shaped by environment and life experiences, then technology, pervasive in our lives as we enter the new millennium, must of necessity have a profound impact on learning preferences both now and in the future.

Marshall McLuhan, once referred to as the "Oracle of the Electronic Age," and formerly the director of the Center for Culture and Technology at the University of Toronto is perhaps best known for his book, *The Medium is the Massage*. McLuhan was a controversial figure, but his contributions to the science of communication were highly acclaimed by popular standards. Much of his theory has significant relevance today as we struggle to weather the transition from an industrial to information-based society.

Here are some of the most relevant aspects of McLuhan's theory:

- Technological media are tools that we build to enhance communication, and these tools, in turn, shape the society that uses them.
- Technological media are staples or natural resources, exactly as are coal and cotton and oil. Anybody will concede that a society whose economy is dependent upon one or two major staples like cotton, or grain, or lumber or fish, or cattle is going to have some obvious social patterns of organization as a result (McLuhan, 1966).
- All media are extensions of our human senses.

With every technological advance, McLuhan's theories reveal how media, as he put it, "work us over completely. They are so pervasive in their personal, economic, aesthetic, psychological, moral, ethical, and social consequences that they leave no part of us untouched, unaffected, unaltered. The medium is the massage."

As the Digital Revolution penetrates our lives, the World Wide Web has unexpectedly renewed printed media... As the Net liberates the book, rejuvenates writing and reading, and makes his vision so clear and sensible. McLuhan's insights carry powerful messages into new environments. It is imperative, as we look at issues related to learning styles, that we consider the impact of Internet and computer technology on learning. Carpenter and McLuhan (eds.), in their book, *Explorations in Communication: An Anthology* (1960), give us a quick look at the "walls knocked over by media change." Here are a few of them.

- Writing on paper allowed for organization at a distance: armies, empires and the end of city walls.
- Print knocked down the monastic walls of social and corporate study. The Bible: religion without walls.
- Print from movable type allowed fast, silent reading and allowed so much information to be made available to individuals that had previously been in the mind and memory of the teacher alone, that it upset all existing educational procedures.
- Print fostered the vernaculars and enlarged the walls between nations.
- It upset the monopoly of Latin by making possible multi-lingual study.
- Print allowed for the molding of public opinion and created a new base for politics.
- The telegraph translates print to sound. It gave us the global snapshot, which knocked out the walls between capitals and cultures, created open diplomacy, or diplomacy without walls.

Before print, the community at large was the center of education. Today, information-flow and educational impact outside the classroom is so far in excess of anything occurring inside the classroom, that we must reconsider the educational process itself. The classroom is now a place of detention, not attention. Attention is elsewhere (Carpenter and McLuhan, 1960).

Since his death in 1980, Marshall McLuhan's reputation has been in hiatus, waiting for electronic reality to catch up. That is happening; a surge of interest in his work emphasizes its usefulness. Not only have his ideas endured, they have retained their primacy in communication theory. Still, no one knows better than he how technology and technological processes transform reality.

As educators in the 21st century, we will increasingly encounter students whose learning styles and preferences are shaped by the technology available to them. Just as print "upset all existing educational process," Internet technology will turn the role of both student and teacher upside down. Both teachers and students will find that the extensions of self made possible by Internet technology will allow students to learn far more independently than every before, and demand that teachers play much stronger roles in helping students to synthesize and evaluate information, rather than just transferring information.

For today's students, the classroom is the world, and the information students have available at the flip of a switch is infinite. We will be looking at this phenomenon in some detail as we explore the learning styles and preferences of generations born between 1920 and 1990.

In the following discussion, we will use the dates that Zemke, et. al. (1999) have used to define the generational groups. There is debate about exactly who is or is not a Baby Boomer and when the first Gen Xers were born. Demographers have defined these groups on the basis of birth rate, and this varies slightly from how others have defined them. (Zemke, Raines & Filipzak, 1999) have based their groupings on psychographics and sociological behavior, thus their dates are somewhat different from those of demographers.

For our purposes, this is useful. As we will discuss, individuals within generational groupings share experiences, perceptions and attitudes that are loosely linked to when they were born. But since generations can span 20 years or more based on birth rate, there will be people at either end of the generation who have very different experiences and therefore different world views.

Even though the Baby Boom spanned the years 1946-1964 based on birth rate, there are adults born before 1946 who consider themselves to be Boomers, and adults born late in this period refuse to be called Baby Boomers because they feel they do not fit the characterization of this group.

It is interesting to go online and visit Baby Boomer sites. The debate is hot and heavy about who is and is not a member of this generation.

Older Adults and Baby Boomers

In spite of the fact that Baby Boomers are loath to admit it, they are rapidly becoming "older adults." In spite of the loudness of their denial, the surreptitiousness of their visits to plastic surgeons and orthopedists, and their bravado, Boomers are getting old. To educators, this matters for a number of reasons.

First, Baby Boomers are inveterate learners. They were the first generation to head off to college is large numbers, and the first generation where women as well as men expected to earn a college degree. According to the College Board, learning begets a desire for more learning. Thus, we can expect that the tendency to learn throughout a lifetime will increase with the Boomer generation. This means there will be a larger number of older adults in classrooms around the world.

Even before Boomers passed over to the dark side of age 50, the older population was increasing. Improved health care and a better understanding of how to maintain a healthy lifestyle have helped to extend the lives of adults well beyond their life expectancy at birth. This generation of older, active adults, and the rapidly aging boomer population will have a big impact on teaching and learning in our society.

Among other things, we can expect to see an increasing number of Baby Boomers among the ranks of mature learners, both in personal enrichment and in work-related classes. They will be there for the same reasons as everyone else:

- They want to upgrade their work skills.
- They are looking for meaningful ways to spend leisure time.
- They are looking for solutions to problems that affect their lives.
- They need to keep up with changes in the workplace.

So far so good... right? Well, let's take a look. For many years, Baby Boomers dominated society and the popular culture as well as the workplace and schools. That generation spanned nearly twenty years — from 1946 to 1964. The first Boomers turned 21 in 1967. The youngest Boomers turned 21 in 1985. Or, to look at it another way, since 1967, the workplace has become increasingly populated by Baby Boomers. In 2006, the youngest Boomers are 42 years old, and although they dominate the adult population in terms of numbers, they are no longer *the* adult population. In the past we, as Boomers have attended classes taught by Boomers, have marketed to Boomers, and have assumed that when we say "this is what people prefer" we are being inclusive. In fact, "people" to us were mostly other Boomers, and we now must come to terms with the idea that other generations of adults may see the world differently from the way Boomers see it. We may have to market or teach differently, depending upon the audience we are serving.

There are several different populations of adults in the workplace and in the classroom now. There are adults older than Boomers - sometimes called the Veteran Generation because they served in WWII. There are adults younger than Boomers, fondly named Generation X because no one knew what else to call them, and already there are younger adults - Generation Y or Millennials.

As people live longer and work longer (Social Security benefits are becoming available later and later) the age diversity in the workplace and in the classroom will become increasingly part of the mix and will increasingly challenge the teachers who will have to teach to a diverse array of multi-generational learners.

This challenge is profound. For years, Gen Xers have been very vocal about their disdain for Baby Boomers, calling them self-centered, egotistical, driven, and over-privileged. In turn, Boomers have labeled Xers as unmotivated, irresponsible slackers with no work ethic. It is not unusual for generations to clash and for generations to misunderstand each other. This has been going on since Adam and Eve. What is unusual, however, is that there is so much age diversity in both work and learning settings.

Further, technology exacerbates the problem. It increases the rate with which new information is generated, and it is the younger people among us who have most fully embraced technology. For teachers, this can pose quite a challenge. Students have access to an infinite information base with the click of a mouse, and have far more resources for independent learning.

Teachers often do not know how to use the technology that their students take for granted. For the first time in history, the technology is pushing us. Because the Internet is open to everyone, and because the Internet is now accessible to more than 60% of people from either home or work, it is increasingly a source of information and a resource for research. Information is no longer a commodity owned by teachers to be given out to students. Young learners today, if they so desire, can move faster than the speed of school. We are truly in a time of great change an uncertainty in our society. This uncertainty permeates every aspect of our culture, but nowhere is it more apparent than in our classrooms.

Adults as Learners

It is entirely possible to have someone in a classroom today who rode a horse to school and received part or all of their education from a single teacher in a one-room schoolhouse. One-room schools were being built as late as 1928, and many operated through the 1950s and early 1960s. In Montana, there were as many as 100 one-room or small rural schools still in operation in 1999-2000 (Fishbaugh, 2000).

Seated next to an adult who went to school in a one-room school house 50 years ago may be a young adult for whom the Kennedy tragedy was a plane crash, not an assassination, and who feels more fear from walking into a school building than from the threat of nuclear war. This student was 11 years old when the Soviet Union broke apart, and does not remember the Cold War. Nuclear war has never been a serious threat for this student. For adults in this age group, "The Day After" is a pill - not a movie. It would be nearly impossible for these two students, with such extremely different backgrounds and life experiences, not to have substantial differences in how they perceive and understand information. It would be nearly impossible for these two learners to not to have differences in how they perceive the learning setting, the teacher, and their responsibilities as learners. And it might be difficult for them to understand each other's values and expectations about life in general, let alone share them.

The fact is that these two learners have grown up in different cultures, in different worlds, speaking different languages, and understanding different realities. These differences will cause them to approach the learning situation differently, and to have different expectations about their roles, the instructor's role, and expected outcomes. For the teacher in our hypothetical classroom, there is a dilemma. How does an instructor serve the needs of both of these very different learners in the same setting? Before we can consider this question, we must first look at some of the characteristics of learners of different ages, and understand the kinds of experiences that have shaped their view of life and their values. Then we must understand how the world view and value issues impact the individual in a learning setting.

Older Adults as Learners

Zemke, Raines and Filipczak (2000) provide some insights into how to understand the differences among the generations, and how to address some of the problems that arise when adults with wholly different ways of working, talking, and thinking are tossed together in the workplace or the classroom.

Chapter 7: The Cohort Experience

In recent years, society has been obsessed with classifying every person into a demographic category. The Baby Boomers, the first generation to have a name all its own, have made headlines for the past 50+ years. As other generations came along, demographers and the media felt it necessary to find a name for every generation. Thus, we have "Depression Babies" (sometimes called "Veterans"), "The Silent Generation (sometimes called the "Lost Generation"), "Generation X" (sometimes called the "Baby Bust"), and "Generation Y" (sometimes called "The Net Generation" or "Millenials").

For all their differences, there is one thing these groups have in common; they all have experienced, as a group, specific events and societal trends which have shaped their behavior, their perceptions of the world, and their values. These specific events are called "cohort experiences," and for each demographic group listed here, there are events and occurrences that have left an indelible mark on the world view of that generation. Because cohort experiences have such a profound impact on generational norms, it seems reasonable that learning styles and preferences as well as other perceptions and values are affected.

In the following pages, we will examine some of the ways in which societal trends have impacted the values of different generations and how they have affected the learning preferences of different generations. These observations have a profound message for all teachers and trainers who want to make sure that their students perform at their highest potential.

Chapter 8: The Veterans (1920-1945)

"We were a 'can do' people who accomplished whatever we set out to do. We had licked the Depression, turned the tide in WWII, and rebuilt Europe..."
— *Doug McAdam, sociologist, early 1960s*

Demographers generally define the G.I. Generation or the Veteran Generation as those people born between 1920 and 1933. The Silent Generation, too young to be soldiers and too old to be part of the Boomer culture, make up the other component of oldest learners, and generally were born between 1933 and 1946. However, since those born at the end of one generation and the beginning of the next often overlap substantially in terms of values and world view, the precise years of birth are less significant than the shared experiences of the cohort's members. The group of adults born during the second half of this period is sometimes called "Depression Babies," and have some significant differences from those born earlier. "The Greatest Generation" is the name given to this group by Tom Brokaw in his book by the same name — and there's no wonder.

This is the generation that survived the depression, won a world war, and shaped the world as we know it today through tough post-war policies. These parents of the Baby Boomers not only raised and educated the largest generation of children in America's history, but also managed to put a man on the moon, wipe out deadly diseases with miracle medicines, and amass incredible personal wealth in their spare time. When we hear talk of returning to "family values," it is a reference to the moral values of the Veteran Generation (Zemke, Raines & Filipczak, 2000). Interestingly, however, it is the younger adults who are returning society to these values — Generation X is leading the way on this issue.

Generational Personality: The Veterans

When we consider this generation, we tend to think of it as the generation that survived the depression and fought in World War II, which is certainly a major influence on the generational personality of this cohort. In fact, however, there are additional societal factors that were at play for this generation and which affected them as profoundly as did the depression and the war.

Some writers, such as Strauss and Howe (1997), have suggested that there are cyclical patterns in generational personality. They suggest that the Millennial Generation (Generation Y) has more in common with the Veteran Generation than with any other, and they point out the parallels between present and past generations in their book, *The Fourth Turning*. These observations are of interest because, in some measure, they support this author's thesis that each generation develops a world view and mindset in response to the social and political dynamics of the world in which they come of age. Let us consider some of the more profound but subtle dynamics of contemporary life during the formative years of those in the Veteran Generation. We will find that there are many parallels in the social dynamics of that generation and the Millennial Generation. Understanding how these societal dynamics affected our parents and grandparents (and for some of us, great-grandparents), we may be able to better understand some of the behaviors of today's youngest generation. They are not their grandparents or great-grandparents, but the same kinds of forces that affected the older generation are affecting today's youth. The behaviors are different because the times are different, but the forces are the same.

The Veteran Generation and the Changing World

"The Greatest Generation" came of age in a world that was profoundly different from the world of its parents and grandparents. Its members were born during a period when the pace of change was unlike anything ever experienced in our history. People were abandoning the farm in great numbers, and they were moving into the cities where new factory jobs promised a higher, more predictable income. The new technologies that made the factory jobs possible, also made it possible for one farmer to effectively farm many more acres than was possible in the past — the gasoline engine made tractors available, and tractors could out-perform the horse or mule and plow. Thus, fewer farmers were needed to produce the nation's food.

Life in the city was remarkably different from life on the farm. New technologies — the automobile, the telephone, the extension of electricity into the rural areas — contributed to changes in life that were as profound as those fostered by the introduction of the personal computer and the Internet.

Not only were America's farmers leaving the farm for the city, but there were also vast waves of immigrants from Europe who were flooding into the United States. These immigrants moved in large numbers into the urban areas of America where jobs were more abundant. This population provided cheap labor for the growing industrial economy of the country, and had a profound impact on the social structure and institutions of the country. From the workplace, to the educational system, to recreational activities, the world was being turned upside down. There were many parallels to our own time — from the movement for "English-Only" instruction in schools, to the fear of loss of face-to-face contact resulting from new technologies which allow everything from business to earning a college degree to be accomplished at a distance, to parents scandalized by the evils of "modern life," there are parallels.

Progressives like John Dewey were concerned with how to intertwine new technology with face-to-face ties. While they recognized the larger, new society, they also cherished the smaller, older social networks of neighborhoods. Dewey wrote:

> The Great Society created by steam and electricity may be a society, but it is no community. The invasion of the community by the new and relatively impersonal and mechanical modes of combined human behavior is the outstanding fact of modern life... The machine age in developing the Great Soci-

ety has invaded and partially disintegrated the small communities of former times without generating a Great Community (Dewey and Lippman: A Comparison).

Mary Parker Follett, another progressive added:

> Real solidarity will never be accomplished except by beginning somewhere the joining of one small group with another... Only by actual union, not by appeals to the imagination, can the... varied neighborhood groups be made the constituents of a sound, normal, unpartisan city life. Then being a member of a neighborhood group will mean at the same time, being a member and responsible member of the state (Follett, 1918).

Not only was there the sense of loss of community that many today fear, particularly in the ongoing debates about the validity of online learning, but there were other parallels, as well. For example, in the realm of professionalization of leisure activities and forsaking participation for spectatorship, there are similarities. In the words of sociologist Robert Park (Putnam, 2000) who wrote in the early 20th century:

> In politics, religion, art and sport, we are now represented by proxies where formerly we participated in person. All form of communal and cultural activity have been taken over by professionals (pp 377-378).

We see parallels in our own time in every activity from music to sports, where playing for fun has virtually disappeared.

Changes in society spawned responses, and the new social structures that evolved had profound impacts on the generational personality of the Veteran Generation. One response of society was a boom in building professional associations.

Some were established between 1865 and 1900, but historians agree that they served the basis for a massive new structure of civic associations in the late 19th and early 20th centuries. This movement spawned many organizations that are still familiar to many of us, but which are today, in a state of decline (Putnam, 2000):

Social Clubs
Service Clubs

Boys Clubs
Girls Clubs
Lodges
Veterans Groups
Professional Associations (National Recreation and Park Association, National Education Association, and many more)

These organizations formed the foundation of 20th century civil society. These were the organizations that were populated and reached huge participation by the Veteran and Silent Generations. Consider those people you know from this generation and reflect upon their current or past civic involvement. The author's father, at the age of 84, is a clear example of this ethic. He has always participated in civic and service organizations. He still actively volunteers. He drives the DAV Van (Disabled American Veterans) to transport veterans to the V.A. hospital. He serves on the town Planning Commission, teaches Sunday School, and until very recently was still active in the Boy Scouts organization. Her father-in-law worked at the local library, volunteered for the scholarship committee at a local college, and delivered meals on wheels. Her mother-in-law fundraises for the local historical association, serves as docent on the museum board, delivers meals on wheels, and is active in her church.

Society in the early 20th century responded to the profound changes of the time in a variety of ways, and it is reasonable to believe that our contemporary time will be no different. The responses will be different than they were 100 years ago, but they will be parallel, and they will respond to the needs of society as effectively and profoundly as they did in the last century.

In the early 20th century, there emerged leaders in every arena of life, from education to politics to social reformers, who became known as the "progressives." The progressives sought to address the social dysfunction that was spawned by the rapid changes in society. The first progressives, figures such as John Dewey in education, Theodore Roosevelt in politics, and Jane Addams in social welfare emerged as leaders in the early years of the 20th century. Interestingly, in the election rhetoric for the 2004 presidential election, Howard Dean, a democrat, positioned himself as a "progressive" candidate — the first time since the progressive movement of the 20th century that this position was put forward as a rallying point

The Measure of Progress

The progress of the past, as well as that of the future, is measured by criticism—for criticism exists only where there is faith in ability to improve.

We do not criticise an ox cart or condemn the tallow dip, for the simple reason that they are obsolete. During the reconstruction period through which our country is now passing, if the public does not criticise any public utility or other form of service, it is because there seems little hope for improvement.

The intricate mechanism of telephone service is, under the most favorable conditions, subject to criticism, for the reason that it is the most intimate of all personal services.

The accomplishment of the telephone in the past fixed the quality of service demanded today; a greater accomplishment in quality and scope of service will set new standards for the future.

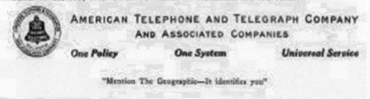

AMERICAN TELEPHONE AND TELEGRAPH COMPANY
AND ASSOCIATED COMPANIES

One Policy   *One System*   *Universal Service*

"Mention The Geographic—It identifies you"

Property of AT&T Archives. Reprinted with permission of AT&T.

for voters. Indeed, he likened himself to the influential and controversial progressive political leader of the early 20th century, Robert La Follett. Regardless of how voters responded to the "progressive" agenda at the beginning of the 21st century, it is likely that as society struggles to adapt to the profound changes of the time, such ideas will establish a stronger foothold in the public mind.

Certainly, progressive ideas were thoroughly entrenched in the last century by 1920, the year that the first members of the Veteran Generation were born. Thus, the members of this cohort became the beneficiaries of these ideas, and their lives and values were shaped in large measure by them. Their generation was the first to experience the full social benefits of progressivism, from the establishment of parks and public playgrounds to the elimination of child labor and the establishment of compulsory education. Following is a statement from Theodore Roosevelt, who not only called for parks within cities, but also succeeded in establishing five national parks during his presidency.

> City streets are unsatisfactory playgrounds for children be-
> cause of the danger, because most good games are against the
> law, because they are too hot in summer, and because in
> crowded sections of the city they are apt to be schools of
> crime. Neither do small back yards nor ornamental grass plots
> meet the needs of any but the very small children. Older
> children who would play vigorous games must have places
> especially set aside for them; and, since play is a fundamental
> need, playgrounds should be provided for every child as much
> as schools. This means that they must be distributed over the
> cities in such a way as to be within walking distance of every
> boy and girl, as most children can not afford to pay carfare
> (Roosevelt, 1907).

For the first time in history, child labor laws were enacted to protect children from hard work in the factories. Compulsory education laws were enacted, and society began to see childhood very differently than in the past. In 1918, for the first time there were more teens in school than out of school, and children were raised in increasingly protective environments. Social chaos in the cities was addressed in a variety of ways; one of the most long lasting and influential was the progressive movement in the schools. One influential model, which was implemented in many communities, was based on the philosophy of Frederick Taylor, who created a system in which children were educated with an intentional goal of socializing them to be productive workers in the country's factories. The most famous of these educational plans was known as the "Gary Plan" which was put in place in the mill town of Gary Indiana (Cohen, 2002). With the stated philosophy of work, study, and play, the schools were designed to look and function like the modern factories of the time. The idea was to replicate the key activities of daily life in proper relationship (work, study, play) and included such innovations as:

- Schedules/bells
- Double shifts
- Focus on efficiency
- Focus on conformity
- Stated goals of assimilation of immigrants
- English only

In one school, which incorporated an indoor swimming pool, the purpose was not primarily for recreation and physical education, but was a surreptitious strategy to make sure that the immigrant children bathed regularly. Schools also were designed to operate with maximum efficiency. For the first time, students moved from one class to another upon the sounding of a bell, maximizing the use of all the available space. In order to make sure that the schools were optimally efficient, a system of shifts was implemented so that the facilities were being utilized for as many hours of the day as possible. Classrooms often resembled the factory floor, and society embraced the idea of an industrial education curriculum that prepared a generation of workers for employment in the factories.

For young women, there was a major emphasis on home economics. These women, upon graduation from high school, or in some cases, the university, undertook the noble charge of helping to assure domestic tranquility through home economics. Not only did they establish their own efficient and supportive homes, but these young graduates were also hired to go into the homes of immigrant women and help educate them in the domestic arts. The prevailing thinking was that if immigrant women were educated in this way, they would be able to provide a more inviting and desirable home life which would be sufficiently compelling to their factory worker husbands that they would by-pass the pubs and the bars and head directly home to a savory meal and adoring family. Such ideas persisted well into the 20th century and illustrate the tremendous pressure that society placed upon school as the solution to the social problems that developed in the beginning of the last century. This writer cannot help but compare this thinking of the early 20th century to the proposition of our President in 2002; that more than 300 million dollars of federal money be earmarked to support the institution of marriage and the family, with a particular emphasis on educating low-income, minority and immigrant women (NPR Morning Edition). This federal initiative would encourage young welfare recipients to tie the knot. Once again, we are seeking domestic tranquility through the home arts.

The schools became centers to provide millions of young people with the skills needed to live successfully in a changing society. The schools that adopted the Gary model were sometimes called "platoon schools," and emphasized conformity, consistency and discipline. These were the behaviors that were rewarded in the factory, and it was important for workers to enter their jobs with the right set of values and skills. On the assembly line, conformity and consistency, not innovation and creativity, were the goals, and that is what was rewarded. Attendance and punctuality were important for the efficient operation of the factory, and these expectations were reinforced early on in the schools.

The children of the progressive era were raised as protected youth. It could be said that childhood, as we understand it today, was invented in the early 20th century. It was an era of prosperity, and new technologies made all manner of new and modern conveniences available. From electric toasters to Electric Victrolas to the automobile, children were exposed to new and amazing machines. Much as today's young people have embraced the digital technology that has emerged with such force, young people of the progressive era embraced all the miraculous machines that science had made possible. They valued the idea that human intelligence could devise such wonders, and in a period of unprecedented prosperity fueled by the growth of industry, the consumer culture that was to characterize later generations... to this day... emerged full-force.

This award was given to students for being "neither tardy nor absent" for an entire school year. The author's father earned 10 of these awards in his 11 years of pre-college education.

One of the interesting paradoxes of the progressive movement was that, although the focus of education was to prepare young people for jobs in a new industrial society, it was also very child-centered. The idea that children learned best when their life experiences were incorporated into the classroom was a key element in progressive educational philosophy. Thus, children in the veteran generation came of age during a period of unprecedented prosperity, in a world where children were at the center of education and social reform, in which stability dominated, optimism about the future ran high, and consumerism reached new heights.

In 1929, things fell apart when the stock market crashed and the world was plunged into a deep, long-lasting, global depression. Thus began the second phase of the "training" that was to have life-long impact on the world view of members of the Veteran Generation. The Great Depression reduced the wealthy to paupers overnight. The protestant work ethic was challenged as it became apparent that hard work did not always equal success, and that poverty was not always caused by lack of effort, work and motivation. Little contributed to the development of patience more than waiting in line at a soup kitchen for a meal or than daily seeking some small job to earn enough money to buy bread for one's family. The lessons of the Great Depression, which left their profound mark on the personality of the Veteran Generation, were patience, persistence in the face of adversity, frugality, sacrifice, conservatism (of resources), and delayed gratification. Remember "lay-away?" This was the "credit" plan for members of the Veteran generation. Subsequent generations, less willing to delay reward, are quite willing to create substantial amounts of personal and credit card debt — a behavior quite alien to their parents and grandparents. While in the minds of many young people today, a coin of any denomination is of no value, for those who lived through the depression, it is still worthwhile to pick up a penny on the street.

The third major life event that shaped the personality of the Veteran Generation was World War II. Their early training in conformity and consistency, stemming from their earliest school experiences, the reinforcement of the importance of persistence and patience, again served them well in times of war. For the G.I.s who fought in both the European and Pacific theatres, these lessons from the past gave them the world view necessary to survive the war. Indeed, the term snafu, meaning a complication or problem, was derived during the war. It is short for "situation normal,

U.S. Government Printing Office posters, on this and the next pages, obtained from Northwestern University Library, http://www.library.northwestern.edu.

all fouled up." Thus, even in the chaos of war, the patience of the armed forces was exemplary. Likewise, a good soldier follows orders. Consistency and conformity are important to an effective fighting force, and World War II forces were well trained in this virtue. The new lesson learned from the war was that of holding close counsel. Both soldiers and civilians alike learned quickly that it was critical to keep any information about military activity completely confidential. The well-known admonition, "Loose lips sink ships," was reinforced both within and outside the military. Further, this post-Victorian generation had internalized some of the formality of their parents, particularly in regard to discussing personal or family matters. Thus, this generation is one whose members tend to be cautious about sharing personal information and talking about personal experiences.

The author's 17-year-old son was assigned to interview a veteran of World War II. He revealed that when he and his classmates reported on their interviews, many indi-

cated that the person they interviewed said that it was the "first time" they had talked about many of the experiences they shared with the young interviewers.

For women, who were the soldiers of the home front, the discipline of living with rationing, shortages, and often juggling wartime jobs and parenthood also created a sense of sacrifice and solidarity. For this generation, much of its greatness derived from the sense of community that came from confronting and overcoming a shared threat.

The Post War Years

After the war, the G.I.'s returned home. They were hailed as heroes, and continued to make one heroic accomplishment after another. Dreaded diseases were conquered. Vaccines were developed that eradicated diseases such as smallpox and ended the threat of Polio. Scientists created rockets that could orbit the earth and ultimately put a man on the moon. Progress again became a cultural icon and science reigned supreme. It was this

world into which the Baby Boom Generation was born, and it was these values — the values of their parents — that profoundly shaped their world view and attitudes.

Perhaps nothing exemplifies the values of this generation better than their beliefs about parenting. For this generation, valuing conformity and structure as they did, it is no wonder that the advice of the best authorities on child rearing, at least up until the advent of Dr. Spock, advised parents to "mind the clock, not the baby."

Babies, the experts believed, needed to learn from their earliest days about structure and discipline. Therefore, babies were fed, bathed, changed, taken outdoors and put to bed on a rigid schedule. If the baby cried between feedings, it was best not to give in and feed him or her, since it was necessary for the baby to learn about delayed gratification. Even in their parenting, families were conforming, structured, and disciplined.

Profile of the Personality of the Veteran Generation

When considering the defining experiences of the Veteran Generation, including:

- · The move from farm to factory
- · The stock market crash
- · The Great Depression
- · The Second World War
- · The Atom Bomb;

it becomes clear why the personality profile of this generation includes:

- • Consistency
- • Uniformity
- • Niftier, new-fangled
- • Conformers
- • Logic, not magic
- • Discipline
- • Law and order
- • Conservative spending
- • Dedication/sacrifice
- • Hard Work
- • Conformity

- Law and Order
- Respect for Authority
- Patience
- Delayed reward
- Duty before pleasure
- Following the rules
- Honor

The Silent Generation

The Silent Generation is a subset of the Veteran Generation. Its members were born too late to have participated in the Second World War, and too soon to have been part of the cultural revolution of the 1960s, which was led by Baby Boomers. Members of this generation, who came of age during the depression and its aftermath (1926-1943), are sometimes referred to as "depression babies."

The Silent Generation is small (49 million members), sandwiched between two much larger and more powerful ones. The Veteran Generation (63 million) and the Baby Boom Generation (78 million) both dominated societal trends, while the Silents had much less influence or impact. Like the middle child, members of this generation developed strategies for success that were quite different from those older and younger.

Often described as a helper generation, today's older adults in the Silent Generation represent a demographic group that has been described as a generation of peacemakers. Coming to maturity between the Second World War and Viet Nam, this generation interceded to try to bridge the growing gap between the elder generation and the baby boomers.

One of the most distinctive qualities of this "peace-maker" generation is its collective concern for others and their plight in life. Called an inclusive generation, many adults in this cohort have high levels of human relations skills. Although they have been criticized as being too tolerant of pluralistic belief structures, this generation has brought about great changes in our collective social conscience because of its pluralistic perspective. The Silent Generation has great potential for changing the world around us and often responds well to efforts that focus on meeting the needs of people (Hanks, 1996). It was this strongly held value that influenced the Baby Boom Generation as its members supported the

7th, 8th, and 9th Months

TRAINING THE BABY

**Parents must work together to teach
the baby good habits**

Weaning—When the baby is 7 months old ask the doctor about weaning him.

For a week give one feeding of cow's milk a day and three breast feedings. (The 10 p. m. feeding can usually be omitted at this age.) Then for 4 or 5 days give two feedings of cow's milk a day and two breast feedings. For the next 4 or 5 days give three feedings of cow's milk a day and one breast feeding. After that (15 to 17 days after the beginning of weaning) the baby should get no breast feedings, but should get four feedings of cow's milk a day, as well as cereal, vegetables, egg yolk, orange juice or tomato juice, and cod liver oil.

Sleep—The baby should have a long morning nap and a short afternoon nap.

Solid foods—If the baby has not yet learned to take solid food, keep on teaching him, giving first the solid food and afterward the milk. Do not worry if he refuses to eat solid food. If you do he will soon learn that he can get a great deal of much-desired attention by refusing to eat.

Toilet Habits—Keep on training for regular bowel movement.

Exercise and Play—At playtime put the baby on a blanket on the floor or in a clothes basket or a play pen and let him learn to amuse himself with simple large toys, such as balls, blocks and boxes.

Tantrums—Do not give in to the baby if he holds his breath or cries, or shows temper in other ways. If he does this, he is already being spoiled.

Sun Baths—Keep on giving sun baths.

BABY'S DIET

Cow's Milk—Each time you leave out a breast feeding give a bottle of milk mixture or of whole milk, whichever the doctor advises. Give the baby fewer and fewer breast feedings as he learns to take cow's milk feedings instead.

Vegetables—Green vegetables should be given every day, 1 to 3 tablespoonfuls (see card for 1 year to 15 months).

Egg Yolk—Give the yolk of a coddled, soft-boiled, or hard-boiled egg every day.

Cereal—Twice a day (10 a. m. and 6 p. m.) give 4 tablespoonfuls of thick, well-cooked cereal, or Pablum or Pabena (precooked cereals).

Cod Liver Oil—1 teaspoonful of cod liver oil (Mead's) daily or 4 drops Mead's Oleum Percomorphum 50% With Viosterol once a day.

Fruit Juice—2 tablespoonfuls of orange juice or 4 tablespoonfuls of tomato juice twice a day.

Water—Offer the baby boiled water, not sweetened, at least twice a day—oftener in summer.

Bread—After the baby's first tooth has come, at meal times give him bread dried in the oven or zwieback occasionally to teach him to chew.

The baby care guidelines printed here are from Dr. L. Nelson Bell, Montreat, NC. They were given to the author's mother in 1943 by Dr. Bell.

10th, 11th, and 12th Months

TRAINING THE BABY

**Parents must work together to teach
the baby good habits**

Feeding—Give up the 10 p. m. feeding. Finish weaning in the tenth month if it is not already done.

Give the baby a drink of milk at 6 a. m. and three regular meals but no food between meals, and no sweets in any form. If he is not allowed to taste candy or ice cream, he will not miss them. Do not give him tastes of food from the family table.

Teach the baby to hold the bottle himself. During weaning it is well to teach him to drink from a cup instead of a bottle. He may begin learning to hold the cup by the end of the first year.

Sleep—Put the baby to bed at 6 in the evening to sleep till morning. The diaper should be changed at 10 p. m. He should still have his regular long morning nap and may need a short afternoon nap.

Toilet Habits—Keep on training for regular bowel movements and begin training for control of bladder.

Exercise and Play—Let the baby learn by himself to stand and walk; do not try to teach him. Let him pull himself up in a play pen or in a crib with high sides. Give him simple toys, too large to be swallowed. Let him find out for himself how to get back toys that he has dropped.

Sun Baths—Keep on giving sun baths.

Protection against communicable disease — Immunization against diphtheria should be started when the baby is 9 months old. Before he is 12 months old he should be vaccinated against smallpox.

BABY'S DIET

Cow's Milk—28 to 32 ounces of boiled whole milk a day, in four feedings.

Cereal and Bread—4 to 5 tablespoonfuls of well-cooked cereal, or Pablum or Pabena (precooked cereals) twice a day. Dry toast or zwieback.

Eggs—Give egg yolk daily, for breakfast or dinner.

Vegetables—4 tablespoonfuls of mashed vegetables daily. Baked white potato three or four times a week.

Cod Liver Oil—1 teaspoonful of cod liver oil (Mead's) daily or 4 drops Mead's Oleum Percomorphum 50% With Viosterol once a day.

Fruit Juice—3 tablespoonfuls of orange juice or 6 tablespoonfuls of tomato juice twice a day.

Cooked Fruit—Applesauce or prune pulp or banana may be given daily.

Water—Offer the baby boiled water, not sweetened, at least twice a day—oftener in summer.

social changes brought about by the civil rights movement, the women's movement, and the peace movement in the 1960s and 1970s. It was the members of the Silent Generation, the tolerant, even-handed, quiet ones that facilitated a change in social values as profoundly significant though far less dramatically visible, as the changes wrought by their predecessors, the Veterans.

The silent generation is also the cohort that led the movement toward early retirement. They were the main victims of the economic downturn of the 1980s, and despite their quiet leadership, they are the only generation that will never have produced a United States president.

Chapter 9: Veterans and Silents in the Classroom

This is a group of "traditional" learners. They are respectful of authority and they want respect in return. They prefer a learning environment that is stable, orderly, and risk-free. Adults in this group tend to be conformers, and they appreciate logic, consistency, and discipline (Zemke, et.al., 1999). They like a traditional classroom and prefer content to be related to real-world practices or supported by precedent (Sensing learning style).

In "Generation Gaps in the Classroom," an article by Zemke, Raines, and Filipczak which appeared in *Training Magazine* in November, 1999, the authors also note that:

- Veterans prefer formality and conservatism in both physical appearance and personal interactions. Anecdotes, stories, and examples that are "too personal" are a turn off. Poor grammar or inappropriate language can make the instructor ineffective.
- Learning is motivated by what is "good for the company" (or family, group, etc.).
- Learning activities that work best for this generation are the straightforward presentation of information and opportunity to build skills privately (Reflective learning style).
- Materials that best suit Veterans are organized in summary form — like *Reader's Digest* or Executive Book Summaries." (Small type is a big no-no, too). Getting the "big picture" first and then moving on to the details is a preference for this group of learners (Global learning style).

When working with learners from this generation, there are some specific do's and don'ts that will help make the learning experience successful:

- Don't do anything that will make them feel "on the spot" in front of peers or younger colleagues.
- Show respect for their background and experience.
- Ask permission to coach or correct. Use tact and show respect, especially if you are a wired twenty-something.
- Develop real-world links and examples for information.
- Make sure that any material to be covered on tests is covered in class.
- Make clear, logical presentations of fact.
- Provide big-picture summaries to be reviewed out of class and also before the beginning coverage of any new materials.

While it is important to understand and respond to the generational preferences of this group in order to communicate effectively, it is also important for younger adults to avoid stereotyping older learners. Keep in mind that this generation is one that values progress, has readily embraced new scientific achievements, and has adopted new technologies such as the automobile, the telephone and television without reservation. It is the generation who first believed and later proved that human beings could travel into outer space. It is a generation that came of age when there was a growing national value placed on learning and education, and these values remain strong among older learners.

With these characteristics, it is no surprise then, that the oldest generation is the fastest growing segment of computer users. One great-grandmother remarked that if her three-year-old grandson could use a computer, then she could certainly do it. (Einhorn, 2004). Other older adults have entered the cyber world in order to keep in touch with their children and grandchildren, to communicate with distant friends via email, and to get the latest updates on health and medical information. While older adults may not be as facile with computers and the Internet as their school-age grandchildren, they are by no means technophobic. In the classroom, it is essential to accept that older learners, with their "can-do" attitude, are willing and able to take on learning with new technology, even if it is a bit more challenging and they are a bit slower in mastering it.

Chapter 10: Baby Boomers (1946-1964)

Never trust anyone over 30.

Boomers are learners. This is the group who wanted more learning after they graduated from college, and who fueled the lifelong learning movement. They have comprised the majority of participants in enrichment and professional development classes, and for the past 25 years have been swelling the ranks of non-traditional students in degree programs as well. As the youngest boomers pass 40 years of age, there is a steady decline in the numbers of non-traditional adults enrolling in colleges and universities. According to the NCES, the number of young students nationally has been growing more rapidly than the number of older students, and this pattern is expected to continue. Between 1990 and 2000, the enrollment of students under age 25 increased by 16 percent. Enrollment of persons 25 and over rose by three percent during the same period. From 2000 to 2010, NCES projects a rise of 19 percent in enrollments of persons under 25 and an increase of eight percent in the number 25 and over (Digest of Education Statistics, 2003).

Boomers are fierce work-a-holics, competitors who are dedicated to success both at work and in the classroom. One of the early readers in the Dick and Jane series, which were the basis of the reading curriculum for most Baby Boomers, was about work. Work was important, and everyone worked. In their book, *Growing Up With Dick and Jane: Learning and Living the American Dream,* Carole Kismaric and Marvin Heiferman (1996) note that the Scott Foresman curriculum was as much about socializing a generation as it was about learning to read. They note that "work" was the 18th word introduced into the lexicon. From an early age, the importance of work was reinforced for young Boomers. In the early reader, *We Work and Play*, it is very interesting to note that in Dick and Jane's world, everyone works. Father works.

"Look Baby. See Spot run. Oh, oh. See Spot work." (*We Work and Play*, 1946)

Mother works. Baby works. Even faithful Spot works. But adults don't play. When the children play, a smiling Mother and Father stand by, beaming and observing. Truly work is an important value for this generation, which is sometimes accused of having invented the phrase, "Thank goodness it's Monday."

"Look, Mother. Look Father. See Jane play. See Baby play." (*We Work and Play*, 1946).

Not only was work introduced as an important value to the young, post-war generation, it soon became apparent that in order to succeed, hard work was a necessity. In the largest population cohort in history, there were not enough seats in college classrooms to accommodate all who wanted to attend. In order to get into college, young people had to be the best, and being the best became an essential part of the work style of many Boomers. Likewise, there were not enough jobs to accommodate all the educated young people who applied for them, and so the Boomer generation developed a very competitive approach to life — one that was based upon hard work.

There is no wonder that younger generations, Gen X and Gen Y find the obsessive work ethic of the Baby Boom generation difficult to understand, and that Boomers might think that, because younger generations have a different approach to work, they are lazy, unmotivated, slackers. In a world which, for Gen Xers, there were not enough young people to fill all the college classrooms that had been built for boomers and where there was not enough young talent for the high-tech jobs at which Gen Xers excelled, there was not the same need for intense competitiveness or obsessive work.

Boomers have a lot of bravado, which is part of their competitiveness — but beneath it all, there runs a vein of insecurity. Boomers have been

Young Boomers filled college classrooms
to overflowing, and their sheer numbers
motivated them to do whatever they could
to become successful and to stand out
from the crowd.

obsessed with the need to prove their worthiness, and their angst has provided a lucrative market for the publishers of self-help books. Classrooms have overflowed with Boomers wanting to learn how to become thinner, to deal with difficult people, de-clutter, learn stress management and medita-tion techniques and master the art of social conversa-tion. Spiritualism has always been important, from the 1960s when young Boomers were ex-ploring alternatives to traditional religion, to now when old Boomers are ex-ploring alternatives to traditional religion.

Boomers grew up in a time when science ruled — men walked on the moon, modern medicine could find a cure for the most dreaded diseases, and there was almost no mystery in the universe that could not be explained by science. In spite of this, or perhaps because of it, there was and remains a deep interest in the spiritual aspects of human existence and in the "unexplainable." Thus, Boomers are in many ways an almost comic contradiction as they search intently and persis-tently for "the meaning of life."

There are some interesting aspects of the Boomer Generation that set it apart. First, Boomers don't believe that they age. In 1996 when the leading-edge Boomers (note, we don't use the term "oldest" Boomers) turned 50, the *New York Times* did an extensive review of this cohort at the mid-century mark. Among other things they found that:

- The majority of Boomers believed that middle age begins at age 72.
- 32% feel they are their chronological age.

- 46% feel they are 10-20 years younger than their chronological age.
- 12% feel older than they are.
- 10% "are always a kid at heart."

  (*New York Times*, January 1996)

If Boomers seemed out of touch with the aging process at 50, it cannot be assumed that by age 60 they would have taken a different view. Lauren Hutton declared on the cover of the March, 2004 issue of the *AARP Magazine* that "60 is the new 30." Thus, it is important when teaching, managing, or communicating with Boomers, to realize that they perceive themselves to be anywhere from 15 to 30 years younger than their chronological age.

Young Boomers filled college classrooms to overflowing, and their sheer numbers motivated them to do whatever they could to become successful and to stand out from the crowd.

And finally, Boomers, like the younger Gen Xers, see themselves as independent and even iconoclastic. Boomers want to stand out from the crowd. They want to demonstrate what they know, and every boomer wants to have positive recognition of his or her uniqueness, talent, skill or accomplishment. This has led Boomers to seek experiences. Boomers are very reluctant to have any weakness or shortcoming made apparent in public — thus, for example, role-play is not a good pedagogical tool for this group. They want their accomplishments to shine and their shortcomings to remain hidden. Additionally, fairness is a big issue with boomers. In a world like the one in which they grew up, where there sometimes had to be losers as well as winners, fairness was essential. If one didn't win, it could be accepted as long as the one who did win did it fairly.

Boomer Cohort Experiences and Generational Personality

In spite of growing up in a highly competitive world, Boomers were also a sheltered lot. They were the recipients of the advances in science and technology developed by their parents' generation, and they were raised in a world where optimism was boundless, and it seemed that science could conquer all. Their fathers had made the world safe for democracy, the economy was booming, opportunity seemed endless, and everything was on track.

Cohort Experiences
- McCarthy hearings
- Rosa Parks
- First nuclear power plant
- Peace Corps
- John Glenn
- Martin Luther King
- Kent State

- Polio vaccine
- Sputnik
- JFK
- Cold War
- Vietnam
- Woodstock

Generational Personality
- Overly sensitive to feedback
- Self-centered
- Don't like authority
- Entitled
- Service oriented
- Willing to go the extra mile
- Want to please
- Not budget minded
- May put process (learning) ahead of outcome (practical application)

- Judgmental
- Over-confident
- Demand fairness
- Self-deluded
- Driven
- Good at relationships
- Good team players

Although Boomers grew up in a competitive world, they were also the most pampered generation to that point in history. They were optimistic, almost beyond reason, and shattered when the first realizations of an imperfect world began to become apparent in their consciousness. The assassination of John F. Kennedy is, of course, indelibly marked in their psyches as a defining experience for most Boomers. Its impact was profound, as young adults became more aware of the inconsistencies between their beliefs and the reality of the world. The gradual unfolding of the imperfection in society led directly to the increased cynicism of younger Boomers and of Generation X.

Boomers in the Classroom

Boomers know a lot. They are achievers, both inside and outside of the classroom, but Boomers have "a tendency to know things intellectually — and remain unaware that they have not translated knowledge into skills." According to Zemke (1999) and his co-authors, many of the following considerations can help assure that Boomers learn most efficiently:

- Boomers are interactive and non-authoritarian. They frequently have good people skills and like to be free to form relationships with their co-learners.
- Boomers respond well to the traditional classroom as long as there is opportunity for interaction, networking, and teamwork (Active learning style).
- Many boomers have authority issues. They didn't like the strict, militaristic, regimen that many experienced during childhood, and they still resent shows of power. Effective teachers will relate to Boomers as equals, not superiors. Boomers like friendly, collegial instructors who share their own vulnerability through anecdotes and examples.
- Boomers are winners. The 2000 presidential election was the first time that two Boomer candidates ran for president in the United States. Although the nation was frustrated with the outcome of the election, and many felt there should have been closure long before things were finally decided, it was in some ways predictable. Boomers play to win, and in the contest between Bush and Gore, both were accustomed to being the winner; it's the Boomer way. In this case, someone had to lose, so it ultimately became an election where some would contend that the loser won and the winner lost. Boomers can be motivated to learn if they believe the knowledge and skills they are acquiring will give them new ways to come out on top — to be the star — to win.
- Boomers value learning for learning's sake. Unlike younger generations who see learning as a tool to be used to achieve a goal, Boomers see learning as an end in itself. It is interesting to note that the vast majority of tag lines or slogans on continuing education brochures developed by or for Boomers include the word "learning." For those brochures targeting younger learners, the word "learning" is conspicuously absent. Tag lines include such one or two word phrases as "Succeed," "Elevate," "Get There," and others that suggest that learning is not an end in itself, but rather simply part of the process. This can also help explain why younger adults have such a different view of school performance. Their goals are quite different. They want to learn as efficiently and quickly as possible only that information that

will bring them closer to an end goal. For Boomers, often the learning itself is an important end goal.

- Interactive activities (icebreakers, team activities, small groups, discussions) are effective with Boomers. But watch out for role-play. Boomers hate it.
- Skill-building, practical activities are very important for boomers because they tend to intellectualize rather than practice. Because of their competitiveness, Boomers don't like to display their shortcomings in front of others, so skill-building activities must be carefully chosen in order to be effective.
- Boomers like materials that are organized in a way that makes information easily accessible. In fact, Boomers will be quick to blame the instructor for any problems they may encounter in the learning setting if they believe the materials are inadequate or poorly presented. The Internet is perfect for Boomer style: overviews of information in an easy-to-scan format with options for seeking more detailed information. Two publications that have a similar format are *USA Today* and *Business Week.*
- Show them that you care. Fairness is big with Boomers.
- Tell them they are important. They're used to being "stars" so they'll want to shine in your classroom.
- Know their names. In the teeming mass of Boomers, everyone wants to have an identity.
- Give them a chance to talk. They will do it anyway, because they all want to show what they know.

More Tips for Teaching Boomers

- Just because you're the instructor, don't think they accept that you're the authority. Dialogue and participation are key for this group. Boomers like instructors who are friendly and collegial and who treat them as equals.
- Don't be authoritarian. Boomers have authority problems, and they'll turn off quickly if they think you're bossing them around.
- Be nice. Boomers value politeness.
- Be democratic. This suggests fairness to Boomers.
- Treat them as "equals." If you don't, they may try to one-up you.
- Respect their experience.

- Acknowledge what they know.
- Treat them as though they're young, even if they're not. Avoid the "sir" and "ma'am" thing. That's an insult to some Boomers.
- Ask lots of questions and acknowledge what they know.

Chapter 11: Generation X (1965-1980)

We are unsettled to the very roots of our being... We are not used to a complicated society. We don't know how to behave when personal contact and eternal authority have disappeared. There are no precedents to guide us, no wisdom that wasn't made for a simpler age. We have changed our environment more quickly than we know how to change ourselves. — **Walter Lippmann, 1914**

Ah, the much maligned generation of thirty-somethings. This generation has a poor reputation which, according to many researchers, is not deserved. In some ways it represents the crux of the focus of this book — the need for generations to understand and respect the styles of those that came before or after them. There is some debate about how to define Generation X. While this author chooses to define generational cohorts by changes in birth rate, which would mean that Gen X spans the years from 1965 to 1980, the period during which the birth rate dropped consistently below four million per year (the Baby Boom) until it once again exceeded four million births per year (Generation Y). Indeed, for many older adults, including Boomers, Generation X is anyone younger than themselves whom they don't understand. One thing is certain about Generation X, however. It is very different from the generations that have preceded it.

Although its members have matured and are no longer in the throes of adolescent rebellion, and although the Mohawk haircuts are gone and the grunge look which they popularized is a faded memory, this cohort is still different, and it is still mysterious in many ways to Boomers and members of the G.I. and Silent Generations. Perhaps M. Hornblower best expresses this in her article "Great Expectations" which appeared in the June 9, 1997 issue of Time Magazine:

> Gen X is not a fad. It is not an aberration, it is not about a generation gone astray. Gen X is about the effects of a changing society on a generation. Those effects are irreconcilable and will affect subsequent generations. If this generation seems 'unmotivated,' or 'without' a work ethic, we must remember that their lack of future expectation is the only sensible stance to take in a world that has proven unreliable, unpredictable, and uncertain and which is now changing at an unprecedented pace.

This generation has not necessarily been well served by the traditional classroom, and its members are not nearly as comfortable in it as preceding generations. It is with this generation that we see a trend that is continuing: the increasing underachievement of boys and a declining number of boys graduating from high school and seeking college degrees. Over the last 20 years — roughly between 1977 and 1997 — among white students the proportion of bachelor's degrees going to males has declined from 55 to 45 percent, and this is similar to the rate of decline for each of the other groups for this same period of time. Census Bureau data indicates that males are less likely than females to graduate from high school at every level of family income, and of those who graduate from high school, males are less likely than females to go on to college in the 18- to 24-year-old age range at every level of family income (Mortenson, *Chronicle of Higher Education Colloquy,* November, 2000).

In fact, this generation has had an uphill climb in many ways. Maligned by older adults as whiners and slackers, and viewed now in the workplace as rude, over-confident, and lacking in social skills, this generation's reality is that their economic situations are very different from those of their predecessors, as is their educational enrollment and attainment. Their media and recreation habits are different, and even their relationships with their parents are different than those of Boomers with their parents (*American Demographics*, April, 1995). It is the Gen X generation who, in a poll of 18-34 year-olds conducted by the 2030 Center, said they do not expect Social Security to pay them full benefits, but nearly nine in ten said that it should. Another poll found that many young adults have virtually given up on Social Security, believing that they will see a UFO before they see a Social Security check (Xavier Becerra, "Social Security is More than a Retirement System," Network Democracy National Dialogue, April, 1999, http://www.network-democracy.org/social-security/nd/rt/becerra_paper.html). While this cynicism may have been dismissed as youthful alienation a few years ago, it is precisely this generation that would be the first to bear the brunt of the Bush administration's proposals for reforming Social Security.

Reading, a favorite recreational activity of Boomers and Veterans, is not as much in vogue with younger adults. Instead, while literature reading has declined among younger adults, the numbers who go to art museums or galleries is increasing. The number who watched a television program or video about artists, art works or art museums totaled 26 percent. The increased interest in the visual arts has occurred in spite of

the decline of formal art education, and some experts say that the pervasive media environment in which today's young people grew up is responsible for their growing interest in the visual arts and graphic design (*American Demographics*, April, 1995).

The photograph on the left provides some good insight into the perception that many older adults have of members of Generation X. The photograph is, in fact, a good lesson in some of the values of this generation.

1. It is highly visual, and the importance of "art" as a personal statement is clearly made.

Body art by Greg "Grease" Lehman, St. Paul, MN. Used with permission.

2. The t-shirt, with its grim statement, "shoot, shoot, shoot, kill, kill, kill," is not, as some think, just another example of the degree to which this "lost" generation has abandoned traditional values. It is an example of how this resilient generation has managed to cope with a world that, in its experience, is unpredictable, unreliable, and unsafe. The statement, as any Gen-Xer will tell you, is a joke. This is a generation that hits issues head-on and sugar coats nothing. It is a recognition of the violence of contemporary society and is a way of dealing with it. Rather than deny it, this generation says, "It's real, so let's laugh about it." Psychologists tell us that often the most horrific events become the source of humor, as is evidenced by jokes that quickly circulate around the Internet following any major disaster. By making light of the unspeakable, human beings are better able to manage their emotions. This t-shirt is just one example.

While many in this generation expressed their adolescent rebellion with elaborate body art and piercing, like human beings have always done, they have grown up. The oldest Gen Xers are now 40 years old and have taken their places as parents and in the workplace. Far from being the turned-off, dropped-out slackers that they were once thought to be, this generation is said by some to be even more motivated than their Boomer predecessors. It is the most highly educated generation in history (Gen Xers are arguably the best educated generation, with 29% obtaining a bachelor's degree or higher: 6% higher than the previous cohort (Schrorer, William, *The Social Librarian,* Generations X, Y, Z, and Others," http://www.socialmarketing.org/newsletter/features/generation3.htm, and National Center for Education Statistics, Digest of Education Statistics, 2003, Chapter 3, Postsecondary Education, http://nces.ed.gov/programs/digest/d03ch_3asp) and its members have the highest percentage of advanced degrees of any generation. Strongly committed to home and family, many Gen X women, in spite of holding advanced degrees, have chosen to be stay-at-home moms, at least until their children are of school age.

Generation Xers are not as attracted to the traditional classroom as their predecessors. It has not served them well. In fact, in 1980 when the first Gen Xers were in their teens, a disturbing trend emerged in the arena of secondary education. Boys began to fail in increasing numbers and with alarming consistency. The number of boys dropping out of school began to climb, as did the numbers of young men going on to postsecondary schools. According to the U.S. National Center for Education Statistics, (Digest of Education Statistics, annual, 1996), the percent of all degrees awarded to men has decreased from 65.8 percent in 1960 to 44.2 percent in 1996. White women earn bachelor's degrees at rates 25 percent higher than men (U.S. Department of Education, National Center for Education Statistics, "Degrees and Other Formal Awards Conferred" surveys and Integrated Postsecondary Education Data System (IPEDS), Table 259, 1976-77 to 1993-94.) and do so in four years or less at a rate ten percent higher than men (U.S. Census Bureau). By 2007, it is projected that women will make up 55 percent of full-time and 71 percent of part-time college students (American Demographics, 1997).

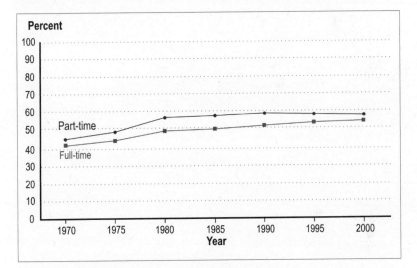

Percent of Female Undergraduate Students by Enrollment Type (US)
SOURCE: U.S. Department of Education, National Center for Education Statistics, Digest of Education Statistics 2002, based on Higher Education General Information Survey (HEGIS), "Fall Enrollment in Colleges and Universities" surveys; and Integrated Postsecondary Education Data System (IPEDS), "Enrollment" surveys.

While the shift in school completion has been most profound for male students, it is this author's assertion that the problems lie not with the students, but with pedagogy that does not meet the needs of contemporary learners. Gen X is the most intensely independent generation in recent history, and its men have taken a stand. If schools don't work for them, they won't work in school. While male students were the first to express their disenchantment with a system that was failing to keep pace with contemporary learning needs, young women have also felt the impact. Although females are more likely to persist in school, there is a definite trend of increasing dissatisfaction with school between both male and female high school students.

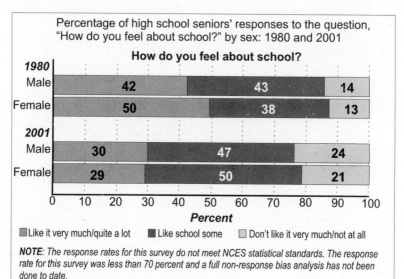

Percentage of high school seniors' responses to the question, "How do you feel about school?" by sex: 1980 and 2001

How do you feel about school?

NOTE: The response rates for this survey do not meet NCES statistical standards. The response rate for this survey was less than 70 percent and a full non-response bias analysis has not been done to date.
SOURCE: NCES "Trends in Education Equity of Girls and Women: 2004: http://nces.ed.gov/pubs2005/equity/Section12.asp

Weekday Readership Consistent as People Age-Life Stage Has Little Impact*		
		Average
Year	Weekday (Ave)	Cohort Age
1979	61%	18-24
1989	59%	28-34
1997	60%	36-42

Reading habits change little with age

Source: From research by Hazel Reinhardt , reprinted courtesy of the Media Management Center at Northwestern University

Newspaper Reading by Generation*		
		Average
	Weekdays	Sundays
Pre-boomers	70%	75%
Baby Boomers	58%	70%
Generation X	47%	62%

Source: From research by Hazel Reinhardt , reprinted courtesy of the Media Management Center at Northwestern University

The Cohort Experience of Generation X

For all of us, our values, points of view, goals and expectations are shaped by our experiences. A great deal of research has been done in recent years, the focus of which has been the brain and how the brain functions. One of the bases for the implications of much of this research is that the brain's main function is to adapt to the environment that an organism or individual inhabits, and to develop responses that are most likely to assure the individual's successful survival.

In today's world, threats, fears, and survival strategies have less to do with how to escape from the threats of predatory animals — the survival challenge of early humans — and more with how to deal with challenges to academic success, social success, and career success. These differences are not taken into account in many ways by our brains. The processes that pilot our survival are still quite similar to the way they were thousands of years ago. Whether a tiger is attacking us or we are experiencing anxiety in a classroom, the brain operates with the same physiological responses. Therefore, it is essential that instructors understand the "survival behaviors" of those whom we find populating today's classrooms. If we think in terms of experiences that lead to behaviors successful for survival, rather than ascribing our own overlay of value judgment to young students, it can be very helpful in creating learning environments that are more responsive to the needs of younger learners.

Most of the defining (as well as daily) cohort events for Generation X were related to a society that was in flux and crisis. Rather than growing up in a world of optimism and belief in an ever-grander future, this generation came of age when many beliefs closely held by preceding generations were under siege. The following are just some of the societal experiences that characterized the lives of Gen X youngsters. The science that was so hopeful for the preceding generation was powerless against the menace of AIDS and the degradation of the natural environment.

If we take a look at some of the events that helped to shape the values of Gen X, what we see is not encouraging. On the personal side, these were "latchkey" kids, left alone after school to take care of themselves and sometimes their families while both parents worked. Huge numbers of Xers were raised in single parent homes, and seeing their parents (some of who had worked for the same company for twenty or thirty years) laid off as businesses downsized, damaged their sense of security.

For Generation Xers, who saw their parents work themselves beyond reason, the idea of all work and no play is not very appealing. They are seeking a better balance in their lives, and some of what Boomers see as lack of motivation is really no more than the desire to keep life in balance and to make sure there is time for fun as well as time for work. Xers see the traditional workplace as unpredictable and unreliable because of the experiences of their parents. Many say that having their own business puts them in control — and many Gen X women are opting to be stay-at-home moms. Because Xers were denied that sense of family, being a housewife is hip.

This is a generation that is often written about as having "survived" tremendous societal stress. Strauss and Howe note that they survived a hurried childhood of divorce, latchkeys, open classrooms, devil-child movies and a shift from G to R ratings. They came of age curtailing the earlier rise in youth crime and fall in test scores - yet heard themselves denounced as so wild and stupid as to put *The Nation At Risk.* As young adults maneuvering thru a sexual battlescape of AIDS and blighted courtship rituals, they date and marry cautiously. In jobs, they embrace risk and prefer free agency to loyal corporatism. From grunge to hip-hop, their splintery culture reveals a hardened edge. Politically, they lean toward pragmatism and non-affiliation, and would rather volunteer than vote. Widely criticized as "slackers," they inhabit a *Reality Bites* economy of declining young-adult living standards (adapted from Strauss and Howe, *The Fourth Turning).* Karen Ritchie calls them survivors of psychedelic parents, divorces, one-parent families, step families, both parents working, razor blades in their Halloween candy, latchkey lives, violence on television, on the streets, and in the schools. This is the toughest generation since the G. I. Generation. (Source: Karen Ritchie, *Marketing to Generation X,* http://chamber.gnofn.org/fishman/xer.html)

From a societal point of view, the failure of the Iran hostage rescue, the scandals of the Clinton Administration and political leaders without integrity, crack, AIDS, gangs, urban deterioration, degradation of the environment, homelessness, the bankrupt social security system, soaring national debt and the increasing fragmentation of communities and families gave them very little to be optimistic about. To the enduring credit of Generation X members, they chose to make light of it all rather than to be overwhelmed. Thus, the irreverent humor so offensive to Boomers, and the disdain for political correctness so valued by Boomers, can be seen to be firmly rooted in the generational experiences of these young adults.

Let's look more deeply at some of the experiences that have shaped the values of Generation X, at some of those values and behaviors, and then at some specific strategies that can help instructors be more successful when teaching students from this cohort.

Political Experience

Quoting again from Professor Brinkley:

The young have few heroes, and they are nonpolitical in the

traditional two-party sense. Weaned on Watergate, on debunked and deposed political candidates, hyena scholars and yellow journalism, the students in my classes tend to admire those who live by what they preach: consumer advocate Ralph Nader, whose austere lifestyle matches his public convictions; former President Jimmy Carter, who takes up hammer and nails to build homes for the poor; Charles Barkley, who sets his own agenda on and off the basketball court; Morris Dees, who takes on bigots and hate groups in the courts. In other words, **respect is granted to those elders who "walk the walk**...

[The] street-wise instinct (of Generation X) is ground in disillusionment with many aspects of American life, an understandable reaction which, in kinder times, would have been praised as **pragmatism.** In our spinning, breathless information society, today's young people embrace deeds, not words; action, not promises. They simply don't want to repeat the mistakes of their parents, and in most circles, this is called **wisdom.** If they appear aloof, it is because they are wary of clichés and propaganda, and because theirs is a legacy of smashed idols. If they seem inclined to take short cuts to reach a desired result, their rationale is that old-fashioned integrity is for those who can afford it.

This is a generation that values humor. With a multitude of experiences that say "having low expectations is necessary for survival" and having lived through parental divorce, corrupt government officials, school violence, drugs, the threat of AIDS and razor blades in the Halloween candy, this group has had two choices — laugh at the absurdity of it all or sink into depression. This resilient group of young adults has chosen the former. Far less self-obsessed than their Boomer predecessors, they are able to laugh at the world around them, and poke good-natured fun at themselves.

Generation Xers don't want "politically correct." That's a Boomer trademark. What they want is the truth, the whole truth and nothing but the truth. They don't want the truth to be candy-coated or diluted or softened to make it easier to swallow. They are remarkable astute and sniffing out what's really going on, so it's best to be direct from the beginning. This website for *Might* magazine is a good example of the kind of direct approach — with humor that gets through to Generation X. As my Gen X son said, "we watched our mothers buy vacuum cleaners that didn't work from door-to-door salesmen wearing plaid sports coats and we're not going to fall for any sales pitches. That's a mistake we're not going to repeat." **They want to know what they're dealing with, and it's best to make that clear up front.**

Social Experience

Generation Xers not only grew up in an era of disillusionment about our political leaders and national heroes, they also grew up with disillusionment about the role of family and community. They were the children of divorce. Single parent families, were standard and new terms such as "blended families" emerged to describe changing family structure and dynamics. If they did grow up in an intact family, chances were strong that they were part of the "latchkey" experience of this generation. With two working parents, which was the norm, having a mom at home with fresh cookies and milk after school was an alien idea. These young people were left to their own devices for many hours a day, and to survive, they developed strategies for managing independently — a characteristic that they carry over into their adult lives. Further, without structure or adult guidance about how to spend time, they developed their own ways of managing — which were quite successful for them, even if they were not consistent with traditional views on the value and management of time.

And finally, there was the great economic upheaval in the late 1980s and early 1990s. These young people experienced first hand the anger and anguish of parents whose loyalty to "the company" was rewarded by a pink slip just weeks before they would have qualified for retirement benefits. They have seen obscene salaries go to sports heroes while they and many others are working for wages that allow only a marginal lifestyle. They have seen huge corporations make sure that the top executives receive financial benefits that will assure lives of ease while workers are laid off with no consideration for their futures. There is no wonder then, that today's young adults scoff at the myth of Horatio Alger, the standard metaphor for America's boundless potential. The only way, writes professor Brinkley, "to go from rags to riches in America," young people say, "is to win the lottery, sue someone, screw over your neighbor or get lucky at one of the nation' proliferating casinos."

The Technology Experience

When Baby Boomers were in school, if a classroom had access to a film projector, that was high technology. The oldest Boomers lived into their teen years without access to television, and radio was the home entertainment of choice. Generation Xers have had a very different experience with technology. Color television was a staple in homes by the time they came along. They learned to read from Kermit the Frog on television, and they are on the leading edge of the computer revolution. While the Internet was not part of their early experience, they have embraced it, as it speaks directly to their experience, needs, and lifestyles. Technology spawned "info-tainment" and "edu-tainment," two words that emerged when this generation was in school. It is not unreasonable to think that these learning approaches are still valued and valid for them as young adults. Thus, if these learners demand a fast-paced, varied teaching approach, it is based on their experiences when they were younger.

Some shared experiences of Gen X:
- Women's liberation demonstrations
- Terrorists at Munich Olympics
- Watergate
- Energy crisis
- Mass suicide in Jonestown
- Three Mile Island
- Massive layoffs (1979)
- John Lennon killed
- Exxon Valdez oil tanker spill
- Fall of Berlin Wall
- Operation Desert Storm
- Rodney King
- Explosion of the Challenger
- Bill Clinton (Monica-gate, etc)
- Stock market crash and recession of the 90s

- Homelessness
- Soaring national debt
- Holes in the ozone layer

Generational Personality of Generation X

- If there is one word that can define Generation X, it is "pragmatic." This generation is extremely practical... as opposed to idealistic.
- Xers value home life and all that goes with it.
  - Gen Xers are family oriented. Their mantra is: "Never confuse having a career with having a life." (Source: unknown) Some 68 percent of married and single women between 18 and 34 prefer the domestic life and aspire to be stay at home moms. (Youth Intelligence, NY). " It's a lot more gratifying to take Johnny to the playground than to haggle with some guy from Tuskaloosa about a late delivery of widgets". The higher you go, the faster you go— competition. Many women want power over their own lives, time, health, and don't want to spend the majority of their waking hours in a cubicle. Jobs will be there when Boomers retire—about when they're ready to come back to work. (Fields, 2000).
- Gen Xers are community builders. Their search for community is evident from their adolescent years and into young adulthood. They formed affinity groups with whom they socialized and who, to some extent, replaced the support traditionally provided by extended and nuclear family. Gen Xers are group oriented. They socialize differently than their elders. The television show, Friends, is an example of the kinds of affinity groups that Gen Xers form.
  - Friends took the place of absentee aunts, uncles, cousins, parents, and even the presence of enough warm, adult bodies in their schools when these adults were adolescents. Going in groups to the malls, group dating, etc., was very natural for this group.
  - Xers have been particularly protective of their groups. The rise of gangs among the most neglected groups of children could be the extreme version of this (Coopersmith, 2000).
- This generation is intolerant of fluff and ceremony. They are direct want information unembellished. They are direct and to the point.

- Gen Xers value efficiency. This generation wants to accomplish the greatest possible amount of work with the least amount of time and effort (not to be confused, as Boomers do, with lack of work ethic).
- Gen X is tolerant of differences. This generation is the most diverse of any preceding generation and is thus more tolerant of differences in race, sexual preference, ethnicity and other differences than preceding generations.
- Gen X is fiercely independent. This is a generation that will do what needs to be done, but will do it in their own way.

Some Shared Views of Generation X

- I want to live comfortably, but I'm not into conspicuous consumption as a symbol of status.
- I know the average college student graduates with about $100,000 in debts. I expect to carry a lot of debt during my life.
- *General Hospital* (soap opera) will still be running when my kids learn about Medicare in History class
- I am working for money, not for fun. I don't expect to enjoy my job.
- I don't necessarily expect to earn as much money as my parents earned. It's a different world, and I won't devote my life to nothing but work. Quality of life is important to me.
- Education is about getting ahead. I'm not interested in "learning for learning's sake." I want to take it to the bank. Otherwise, I'll choose other ways to have fun than sitting in a classroom.
- I'll see a UFO before I ever see a Social Security check (Hornblower, 1997).
- Family is important. Having time at home, even if it means making less money, is a priority for me.
- Community and neighborhoods are important. I want to know my neighbors and be part of a community. I don't like living next door to people who are strangers to me.

Generation X in the Classroom

The "problem" with Generation X members is that they're unmotivated. They don't show up to class unless they feel like it. They don't do the homework. They are not respectful of the instructor. They want to be entertained... in short, they have "an attitude."

This litany of complaints about Generation X goes on and on. Whatever happened to young people to make them so difficult, so different, so impossible? "Whatever it was, it's not our fault," say the parents — the Boomers and Silents who raised these children to adulthood. "Their behavior certainly doesn't reflect our values and beliefs." So if it's not the fault of the older generations, then it must be the fault of the young people who comprise this generation. After all, it makes sense that we would produce a generation of ne'er-do-wells who drop out of college, don't work full time, and live in a world where time and space have totally different meaning than it does to the rest of us, devoid of work ethic and disengaged from traditional societal values — doesn't it?

Wrong. It makes no sense at all, and in fact, we have not produced such a generation — ever in our history. What we did "wrong" with this generation is nothing. What happened to produce this generation is simply life. There is a growing awareness of generational differences in our society. Until quite recently, American society had been dominated by one large generation — the Baby Boom. Consumer products and marketing strategies as well as curriculum and instructional design were created to respond to the behaviors and preferences of this generation.

This generation has been dismissed by its Boomer predecessors as composed of slackers, whiners, and as having a poor work ethic. They have been described as lazy, uncooperative and negative. Boomers characterize them as wanting to "start at the top" without having to "pay their dues." Much has been made of their choices for individual expression, such as body art and body piercing. We are going to take a closer look at this generation of young adults, and hopefully, we'll come away with a better understanding.

When, after 20 years, another generation comes along behind the baby boomers with a different set of motivators, expectations and behaviors, we all throw up our hands in frustration at their lack of civility, work ethic and sense of community. The reality is quite different. The Time Magazine "American Dream Study" done in the late 1990s, has found that this group of young adults is highly motivated, has a strong work ethic, is committed to traditional family values, and is very achievement oriented.

Professor Douglas Brinkley teaches a college credit course at Hofstra University called "American Odyssey: Art and Culture Across America." He and about 30 students spend ten weeks traveling America by bus, studying the nation's heritage and experiencing its diversity. He comments, in his paper called "Educating the Generation Called "X", that "if my students have taught me anything, it is their loathing of the label 'Generation X', which they feel stigmatizes them. 'We're not all watching MTV,' he quotes a 25 year-old-marketing consultant as saying. 'We don't even consider ourselves a generation.' "

This observation is an important key to understanding this cohort of young adults, and understanding is essential to effective teaching. Professor Brinkley notes that "The educator has [a]... duty to reach out and understand the students' points of view, and not try to force them into some procrustean bed of preconceived notions of learning, for there have always been generational differences between the teacher and the taught."

Thus, I submit that in order to effectively teach students in any generation, including Generation X, it is important to "start where they are" and to understand their points of view, values, goals, and expectations for the future.

What this means in your classroom

By understanding the values of this generation, you can become more effective in your teaching: Here are some suggestions that you might consider:

1. Gen Xers want to know, from the outset, what is expected of them. It is important to clearly specify your goals for the class, have a syllabus that outlines the content and includes any deadlines you may have. If you don't include this up front, this group may feel that you are unjustified in imposing it later - because they want to manage their time, and it is your obligation to let them know well in advance what they need to do.

2. Allow choices and options. This group of independent and pragmatic learners may bristle at rigidity. It is important to allow as much choice as possible in determining how to learn material and in assessment strategies.

3. Be efficient and non-bureaucratic. "Wasting time" is a taboo with this generation. Going through unnecessary steps, doing it because

it's "just the way it's done" are not persuasive with this group. Focus on outcomes, not processes.

4. Be relevant. This is a group with very low tolerance for anything that seems irrelevant. Because of their pragmatism, this group is not likely to respond well to anything that seems to serve no purpose toward meeting their educational goals. If you see it but they don't, then you need to make sure they understand it, too.

5. Work to make the classroom come alive. Take field trips, assign self-directed projects and discussion, and develop participatory learning activities. Again, Professor Brinkley notes, "The basics are invaluable, but why not break up the monotony with some participatory learning?"

6. If you have a classroom full of Xers, incorporate humor into your presentations. It will pay off with increased attention, appreciation for what you have to say, and positive attitude towards learning. This does not mean you have to become a stand up comedian. Just not being "uptight" may be enough. Remember, these students don't expect you to be like them, they just want you to understand them and respect them.

7. Be visual. Remember, this group of students learned to read from Kermit the Frog, dancing with the letter "e." Research on learning styles has shown that the majority of students in your classrooms are visual learners. While visual learning is preferred more consistently as age declines, even the majority of older learners prefer visual learning. Possibly, the preference declines with age because older learners have had more time and experience, and have developed other ways of learning that also serve them well. Their experiences with visual learning are more limited than those of younger learners. Indeed, research shows that the common experiences of playing video and computer games that are shared among young people today (especially boys) do increase the strength of the visual learning preference and skill.

8. Use technology. Technology is essential in today's classroom. At the turn of the last century, pencils were an innovative technology. Just as no student in 1900 wanted to use a slate and chalk at school when pencils and paper were available, no student today wants to learn in a classroom dominated by outdated technology.

Integrate the Internet into your classroom. Streaming media presentations and other technological strategies will be valued by your students. If you are not a technological wizard yourself, engage the support of your students to help you. They will be flattered, willing and positive.

9. Use color, novelty, and contrast in your presentations. According to recent brain research, our brains have a built-in attentional bias toward novelty and contrast. The use of computers and technology has not created this bias - it has existed since the human brain evolved. However, these technologies do allow us to address these preferences in positive ways that can enhance learning.

10. Allow frequent breaks, and encourage play. This does not mean that you have to have lengthy breaks every half hour. Based on current research about the brain, Eric Jensen (1998) notes that the maximum amount of time the brain can spend in uninterrupted focus on new content is about 10 to 15 minutes. Then, he notes, the brain needs to take a break. Because we process information visually, the brain needs a little time to translate the verbal/cognitive information that it is taking in into visual images, and to integrate them and assign meaning to them. Thus, allowing a few minutes every hour or so is essential to optimal learning. Other research has found that mice improve their learning if they are trained for short periods and then given intervals of rest.

LERN presenters use a technique called "Outbursts," based on the popular parlor game. In this exercise, the class is divided into groups. Each group is given one minute to create a list of items specified by the instructor, such as ten things that people do in a car. Then the instructor reads his or her list, and those who have the most items that are included on the instructor's list "win." The whole exercise takes about two minutes, uses a part of the brain that is different from the one that has been used in the instructional activities of the classroom, allows some integrative time, and increases learning and satisfaction with the class.

11. While Gen Xers are hard workers, they are not obsessed, like Boomers, with being the best. Boomers will go far beyond what is required in a work or classroom situation. Gen Xers will meet the requirements at a competent level. Being the best is not as impor-

tant as doing a good job and moving on. This represents one outcome of a different orientation to time. Gen Xers don't want to spend a lot of time on over-performing. This simply means that time is lost that could be put to some other valuable purpose (including recreation, family time, etc).

12. Another outcome of the lack of obsession with being the best is that grades in school no longer carry the motivating value they once did. For Boomers, getting A's was essential. In an online class taught by the author on generational learning, students who are Boomers will request an opportunity to re-take a test or rewrite a paper if they earn a B+. Younger students almost never want to redo work if they make a C or better. Boomers see this as lacking in motivation. Younger people see it as efficient.

13. This generation learns best when given a chance to sample and learn by doing. Unlike Boomers or Veterans, they are not concerned about putting themselves on the line. This generation is actually more self-confident than Boomers, and role-play techniques work well. This group does not mind trying something, even if they look clumsy in front of others.

14. This generation wants practical outcomes that will put them ahead or help them achieve a goal. The process of learning is far less important than whether the learning takes them to a higher level of success, which is usually defined in terms of income. Boomers like to intellectualize. Gen Xers like to "do."

15. This is not a generation of readers, and the most effective materials are those that are highly visual as opposed to being heavy with text. Lots of visual stimulation is important for this group. When writing course materials for Generation X, remember that they are used to scanning large amounts of information and gleaning what is important. Provide lots of white space. Use bullet points. Summarize material with all the key points, and then provide additional information for those who want to go further. An example of this occurred in a recent institute in which this author was teaching a one-week course on needs assessment. About mid-point in the course, the participants were asked for feedback on whether the content was meeting their needs. One participant, a Gen-Xer, smiled sheepishly and admitted that she "had not read" the promotional brochure and

really didn't know what the institute included. She had scanned, read the headings, and made some assumptions about content. She further noted that her boss, a Boomer, had read the entire brochure and had virtually memorized the agenda for the institute in which she was participating. Her advice to us was to make the content more visual, use more bullet points, make sure that the most important information is easy to find and is up front. Further, she advised, don't include extraneous information that is not necessary to know in order to make a decision about participation.

If you employ these strategies and understandings in your Gen X classroom, your students are likely to be more engaged, and their learning is likely to be more successful. Remember, too, that every generation is different. The essential tip is to understand these learners and to respect them as individuals.

Generation X is a generation that is experiencing the brunt of change in our transition from an industrial society to an information society. For those of us who find it challenging, it is important to remember that for this group, the challenges are even greater. Their world is one without precedent. More than anything, Generation X is about the effects of a changing society on a generation. Those effects are irreconcilable and will affect subsequent generations (Hornblower, 1997).

Chapter 12: Generation Y (1980-2000)

"... The Millennial Generation will entirely recast the image of youth, from downbeat and alienated to upbeat and engaged — with potentially seismic consequences for America." — Howe and Strauss, Millennials Rising, 2000.

Generation Y is the youngest group of adults in college classrooms and workplace training rooms — and yes, its members are different. They are different from Boomers and Gen Xers, and they are different from older generations as well. This group is also known as The Net Generation, for obvious reasons, or as Generation Next, N-Gen or the Millennium Generation.

They do have a great deal in common with their grandparents and great-grandparents in the G.I. generation, however. Here are some of the parallels:

1. Both generations were born at the end of one century and the beginning of another.

2. Both generations experienced coming of age completely within the period when the country was moving from one era to another. In the case of the G.I. Generation, it was the move from the agricultural age to the industrial age. In the case of Generation Y, it is the movement from the industrial to the information age. (Source: *Nine Shift*)

3. Both Generations experienced radical, new, world-changing technologies (the gasoline engine in the early 1900s and the Internet in the early 2000s). (Source: *Nine Shift*)

4. Both generations are larger than the preceding one.

5. Both generations have been the focus of doting parents concerned about providing them with every advantage.

6. Both generations have come of age at a time when the education system lagged behind societal change. (Source: *Nine Shift*)

7. Both generations see themselves as powerful and able to change the world.

8. Both generations have an optimistic outlook.

9. Both generations have experienced and believe in the power of science to conquer the unknown.

10. Both generations set the stage for the evolution of the next 100 years. (Source: *Nine Shift*)

If, as we have stressed in the pages of this book, the values, attitudes, perceptions and behaviors that are dominant within a generation derive from the shared experiences of that generation, then it is not surprising that Gen Y members, as many have asserted, have more in common and find more affinity with their World War II era grandparents and great-grandparents than with the two generations immediately preceding them.

Gen Y: The Cohort Experience

Generation Y is vastly different from previous generations — especially Boomers. Members of Gen Y cut their teeth on computer keyboards, and to them, computer technology and the Internet are as natural as breathing. This generation's members know more about digital technology than their parents or teachers, and this promises to change not only the ways families interact and communicate, but also how young people relate to schools and learning.

The first members of this cohort arrived when "Baby on Board" signs appeared. As abortion and divorce rates ebbed, the popular culture began stigmatizing hands-off parental styles and recasting babies as special. Child abuse and child safety became hot topics, while books teaching virtues and values became bestsellers. Today, politicians define adult issues (from tax cuts to deficits) in terms of their effects on children. Hollywood is replacing cinematic child devils with child angels; cable TV and the Internet are cordoning off child-friendly havens. While educators speak of standards and cooperative learning, school uniforms are surging in popularity. With adults viewing children more positively, U.S. test scores are faring better in international comparisons (adapted from Strauss and Howe, *The Fourth Turning*, 1997).

According to Ron Zemke, Generation Y combines the can-do attitude of the Veterans, the teamwork ethic of Boomers and the technological savvy of Generation X. For this group, the preferred learning environment combines teamwork and technology. In a classroom with lots of Gen Ys, give everyone a task. When a few have completed it, encourage them to walk around the room and help others. They're used to working this way in school.

Generation Y is the most diverse generation in history. Members are born to the most diverse mix of parents in history as well — from teenagers to middle-aged moms who postponed childbearing to establish a career — from Boomers to Xers. One third of this generation was born to single, unwed mothers. This generation is less white and more brown than any generation in our history, too.

Many of the parents of Gen Ys are mid-life Boomers, used to winning and achieving. Gen Y members have come of age in a very child-focused world. Many of them had Boomers as parents, and Boomers are as competitive for their children as they were for themselves. Boomers are used to getting their way, and they have been strong advocates for their children. Because Boomers have worked long hours, because of many single parent families, because of an increasingly violent world and because of the desire for their children to "get ahead," Boomers have made sure their children participated in all forms of lessons and activities. Thus, Gen Y has grown up in a very structured, busy and over-planned world.

Their children have been the recipients of parenting with zeal unknown in the annals of child rearing. Their parents are "determined to do the right thing, going at child rearing with all the intensity and energy with which they've tackled everything else in their lives. These Boomer parents have a history of getting what they want. If it's happy, well-educated, well-adjusted children they want, it's likely they'll get just that or drive the world crazy trying" (Zemke, et. al., 1999). The result is that Generation Y is made up of confident, optimistic young people who feel valued and wanted.

This generation is almost as much at the center of media attention as were Boomers because their numbers are as great (or even greater according to some demographers). They are projected to comprise at least one-third of the country's population when all is said and done. Their parent's generation, large and powerful, never comprised more than a quarter of the population. Gen Ys are technologically sophisticated, have positive expectations and a bent for collective action. They are bound to influence the 21st century as profoundly as the Boomers influenced the 20th century (Zemke, et. al., 1999).

In "Millennials Thriving: The Colgate Scene," Rebecca Costello wrote that "they're conventional. They're confident. They're special. Sheltered. Pressured. Achieving. Team Players." They also, she notes, "exhibit many positive social habits that defy the traditional wisdom about what makes young people tick." Here are some of the characteristics that Costello has identified for Generation Y:

1. Closer relationships with parents.
2. Admiration for their parents (33% named one or both parents as their hero, rather than a pop culture celebrity).
3. A closer sphere of influence — a more dangerous world has created an environment which is more sheltered and structured, and where young people have been more protected.
4. The smaller sphere of influence has contributed to the creation of a generation that is, in general, more polite and considerate than their predecessors. They are less likely to call adults by their first names, but rather use the more formal Mr. or Mrs.
5. Attentive and respectful, this generation has been brought up to show respect for others. In a crowded world where there are larger numbers of people in classrooms and activities, civility becomes essential to getting along.
6. Programmed and team oriented. According to Costello, some college administrators believe that many Gen Ys have "lost the sense of pure play." They expect everything to be planned for them and do not expect to have as much freedom — or responsibility for structuring their educational lives.
7. Having spent a large percentage of time in structured activities, they are accustomed to having a lot of adult supervision. Thus, they may have poor conflict resolution skills.

8. Pressured to succeed. The Boomers, parents of the Gen Y generation, pressured themselves to succeed and also transferred that pressure to their children. In addition, just as the Boomers lived in a world where there was increased competition for resources, Gen Y has done the same.

9. Involved. This is a generation of activists — young people who believe they can make a difference.

10. Egalitarian. This cohort often prefers to work in teams or groups. They definitely do not prefer hierarchy. Sometimes, according to Costello, faculty finds the lack of authoritarian hierarchy in their groups to create some ambiguity when it comes to having a point of contact for information.

11. Open and eager. Members of Gen Y are very open and eager. Students are responsive and "very smart" according to some faculty quoted in Costello's report.

12. Demanding of themselves and others. Members of this cohort set the bar high for themselves, and they, like their Boomer parents, expect success. They sometimes "expect" to get good grades and are upset when this does not happen.

13. Stressed. Compared with five years ago, 81 percent of college mental health service directors reported an increase in students with serious psychological problems. Pressure to succeed is one reason identified by some counselors.

14. Multi-taskers. This generation can easily manage to listen to music, work on the computer and watch television at the same time. This means they need a lot of stimulation in their learning environments and may be more focused than it seems to their teachers.

15. Socially conscious. There has been a resurgence of interest in politics and social issues. Administrators at Colgate University reported that 70 percent of first-year students came to campus already registered to vote. Some 93 percent indicated that they voted in the 2004 presidential election.

Shared Experiences of Generation Y

- Child focus (Sylvan Learning Centers)
- Oklahoma City bombing
- Busy, over-planned lives (more than 75% of time spent in structured experiences)
- Stress
- Malfunction at Three Mile Island nuclear plant caused a near meltdown.
- Iranian students took 66 people hostage at the U.S. Embassy in Tehran.
- U.S. boycott of Olympics in Moscow
- President Regan shot
- The Equal Rights Amendment passed (though not ratified)
- The Space Shuttle Challenger exploded shortly after liftoff, killing all seven astronauts on board.
- The Exxon Valdez spilled more than ten million gallons of oil in Prince William Sound.
- The Berlin Wall demolished
- Persian Gulf War
- Four white police officers accused of beating Rodney King were acquitted, Shootings at Columbine High School in Colorado left 13 students and one teacher dead; The Dow Jones Industrial Average closed above 10,000 for the first time.
- It took more than a month to declare a winner of the presidential election because of ballot ("hanging chad") disputes.
- Four U.S. planes were hijacked in attacks on the World Trade Center and the Pentagon, killing more than 3,000 people and leading the U.S. into an ongoing fight against terrorism.
- The Space Shuttle Columbia exploded upon re-entry into the Earth's atmosphere, killing all seven astronauts on board.
- The U.S. and Britain declare war against Iraq.

Characteristics of Gen Y

- Bigger than Baby Boom Generation
- 3 times the size of Gen X

- Roughly 26% of population
- Diverse
- Inclusive
- Powerful
- Weak on interpersonal skills
- Cyber
- Activists
- Support social causes
- Impatient
- Active/hands-on learners
- Use technology
- Spending power exceeds $200 billion
- Independent
- Strong Views
- Close to family

Sources: American Demographics, U.S. Census Bureau, USA TODAY research

Following are some real-life examples of how young adults today approach the world and act on their values:

Activist: Jasmine McCoy was a teenager in Asheville, N. C. where teens believed the limits set by a local mall, on the numbers of youth who could be together in groups in the mall and a minimum age at which young people could shop without an adult, went over the line. McCoy, 18, and her friends in the Buncombe County Youth Organizing Project distributed fliers and held meetings during school lunch periods, seeking others with concerns about mall policies. The youth group persuaded the mall to drop its no-bandanna policy and ease the restriction on teens congregating. Asheville's students mirror the views expressed in the USA WEEKEND Teens & Freedom survey: Most teens nationwide said they should be allowed to go to the mall at age 13 without a parent.

Generation Y is not going to think like Generation X, either. Susan Mitchell, author of "The Official Guide to the Generations" writes, "Look at the malls. A few years ago there were fewer teenagers and they kept to themselves. It was kind of sad. But kids aren't hiding off in the corners so much now. They're loud and they're boisterous. They're taking over."

In Asheville, making the mall more welcoming was just one hurdle Jasmine cleared. She was captain of Erwin High School's cross-country and indoor/outdoor track teams this year. She also helped revive the youth chapter of the Asheville NAACP, and was elected vice president. "I've always been a real opinionated person," Jasmine says. "Everybody should have the same rights." (USA Weekend, "Teens and Freedom," May 1997, http://www.usaweekend.com/97_issues/970504/970504teen_mall.html)

Socially Conscious: Kids For A Clean Environment, Kids F.A.C.E.®, is the world's largest youth environmental organization - much more than the first six members who gathered at Percy Priest Elementary in Nashville, Tennessee in 1989. At 9 years old, Melissa Poe started the club for kids after seeing a program on TV, *Highway to Heaven*. She said it made her think, "What will the future world be like if we don't help take care of the environment today? I didn't want to grow up in a world with a polluted environment. At the end of the program, however, Michael Landon, the actor, said something very important. He said, 'It's not too late. People who *care* will Do something!' I wanted to be one of those who 'Cared', and so I started the club, Kids F.A.C.E. as a club for kids who wanted to be involved" (http://www.kidsface.org/).

Now in her early 20s, Melissa still runs the organization and has mobilized more than 300,000 young people around the world in the effort to clean up the environment. She travels internationally, speaking on the topic of environmental conservation. (http://www.leadershiponlinewkkf.org/stories/melissa_poe.asp). For more information on how teens are exhibiting leadership globally, visit www.leadershiponlinewkkf.org.

Cyber: Generation Y is the first real cyber generation. Its members are much more fragmented and much less homogenous than were Boomers. They have been given much more choice. Don Tapscott of Toronto, Canada has written a book called "Growing Up Digital." In it he says, "Choice is like oxygen to them. They're used to customizing everything. And the feedback they get is instantaneous." This is the generation that can go online and customize everything from the music they listen to, to their computers, to their cars. They make or alter their own clothes, and in a commercial for Campbell's Soup, even customize their soup.

This is a group that grew up with CD players, VCRs and computers. Cell phones and palm pilots are par for the course, and even some middle school students use laptop computers. When using technology in instruction, it is important to have, insofar as possible, state-of-the-art equipment. And even more important is that, when using technology, the instructors must really know their stuff, or the students will run circles around them. While Gen Y is likely to be more tolerant than Gen X of instructors who are not up to snuff with technology, they are still likely to be put off by it.

Here are some examples of three young Internet entrepreneurs and the world they have mastered — before they were old enough to vote. Donald Amboyer drives a new car, wears expensive clothes, and owns a home — and he is an 18-year-old computer wizard when all this comes to pass. He uses his handsome salary of $60,000+ per year to purchase his assets. He began working with computers at age 6, and at 18 was working as the director of architecture and development for the Ultimate Software Group, Inc. His job was to create and maintain Internet systems for the company and to develop payroll software for its HR department. In 1998, he began working with Ford Motor Company Credit division, setting up a web site to assist potential customers in acquiring car loans. And this is just "the early years." Amboyer has observed that his high school years were difficult, and that his grades were not great, and he says, as do many in his generation, that he needed to improve his social skills.

Amboyer is not terribly unique in his generational cohort. For example, Brad Ogden, at age 17 worked running Virtual WebPages, a company that sets up Web pages and acts as a network consultant for businesses. Steve Kirka founded SK Computers Corporation at age 13 with $20 and the computer his grandparents gave him as a birthday gift. At age 16, his company was generating a six-figure income, with Kirka managing a staff of 12. There are many other stories that demonstrate the independence, technological skill, and learning ability of Generation Y. Try to imagine, if you will, having a few of these young people in your classroom. (Peter Robbins Brown, http://www.metrotimes.com/20/07/Features/wdKids.htm, "Computer Kids" Source: Wired Detroit 11/17/99)

Mindset 2008

Because this generation is large, sophisticated and influential, much as Boomers were, it is especially important to examine how they will respond as learners. One thing we know for sure is that this group, like every other, has a unique set of values and views of the world.

Beloit College assembled a list of ways in which entering first-year students differ in their frame of reference, not only from their teachers and advisors, but also from those just a few years older than themselves. Here are copies of the annual "Mindset" list created by Beloit College to help faculty better understand the world view of incoming freshmen.

> First-year students (those formerly know as freshmen) are descending on the campuses of America, loaded with cell phones, Palm Pilots, CD burners and other essential items, hardly even imagined a short time ago. They are prepared to dive into courses taught by wise and "all knowing" faculty who may be ten or 50 years their senior (Boch, 2000).

> Each generation has its particular set of cultural icons and touchstones that are critical to its identity. Today, however, the gap in understanding between generations increases dramatically as television, films, vocabulary, and technology adjust the way we perceive and express ideas at an increasingly rapid rate.

> This year's first-year students, members of the Class of 2003, were mostly born in 1981, the year that USA Today hit newsstands and CNN provided us with a revolution in the way we look at the world's events. They have had Sony Walkmen, PCs, NutraSweet, and AIDS around them all their lives.

> "This is not meant to be serious research," notes Beloit College institutional researcher Richard Miller. "The list is collected from suggestions, contributions from faculty and staff, student contributions and questions, and reading old newspapers."

Public Affairs director Ron Nief, who, along with Mr. Miller, assembled the document, notes that reaction to the list in the past has been split between the 19- to 20-year-olds, and their parents and mentors. "The older crowd thinks it fascinating that people don't know what is part of their cultural understanding. First-year students have occasionally expressed surprise and annoyance at some of the suggestions in the list... the availability of cable television and their access to the Internet make more information available to them."

This year's list contains 50 items.

BELOIT COLLEGE'S MINDSET LIST®
FOR THE CLASS OF 2008

1. Most students entering college this fall were born in 1986.
2. Desi Arnaz, Orson Welles, Roy Orbison, Ted Bundy, Ayatollah Khomeini, and Cary Grant have always been dead.
3. "Heeeere's Johnny!" is a scary greeting from Jack Nicholson, not a warm welcome from Ed McMahon.
4. The Energizer bunny has always been going, and going, and going.
5. Large fine-print ads for prescription drugs have always appeared in magazines.
6. Photographs have always been processed in an hour or less.
7. They never got a chance to drink 7-Up Gold, Crystal Pepsi, or Apple Slice.
8. Baby Jessica could be a classmate.
9. Parents may have been reading The Bourne Supremacy or It as they rocked them in their cradles.
10. Alan Greenspan has always been setting the nation's financial direction.
11. The U.S. has always been a Prozac nation.
12. They have always enjoyed the comfort of pleather.
13. Harry has always known Sally.
14. They never saw Roseanne Roseannadanna live on Saturday Night Live.
15. There has always been a Rock and Roll Hall of Fame.

16. They never ate a McSub at McD's.
17. There has always been a Comedy Channel.
18. Bill and Ted have always been on an excellent adventure.
19. They were never tempted by smokeless cigarettes.
20. Robert Downey, Jr. has always been in trouble.
21. Martha Stewart has always been cooking up something with someone.
22 They have always been comfortable with gay characters on television.
23. Mike Tyson has always been a contender.
24. The government has always been proposing we go to Mars, and it has always been deemed too expensive.
25. There have never been any Playboy Clubs.
26. There have always been night games at Wrigley Field.
27. Rogaine has always been available for the follically challenged.
28. They never saw *USA Today* or the *Christian Science Monitor* as a TV news program.
29. Computers have always suffered from viruses.
30. We have always been mapping the human genome.
31. Politicians have always used rock music for theme songs.
32. Network television has always struggled to keep up with cable.
33. O'Hare has always been the most delay-plagued airport in the U.S.
34. Ivan Boesky has never sold stock.
35. Toll-free 800 phone numbers have always spelled out catchy phrases.
36. Bethlehem has never been a place of peace at Christmas.
37. Episcopal women bishops have always threatened the foundation of the Anglican Church.
38. Svelte Oprah has always dominated afternoon television; who was Phil Donahue anyway?
39. They never flew on People Express.
40. AZT has always been used to treat AIDS.
41. The international community has always been installing or removing the leader of Haiti.

42. Oliver North has always been a talk show host and news commentator.
43. They have suffered through airport security systems since they were in strollers.
44. They have done most of their search for the right college online.
45. Aspirin has always been used to reduce the risk of a heart attack.
46. They were spared the TV ads for Zamfir and his panpipes.
47. Castro has always been an aging politician in a suit.
48. There have always been non-stop flights around the world without refueling.
49. Cher hasn't aged a day.
50. M.A.S.H. was a game: Mansion, Apartment, Shelter, House.

Although these lists are intended to be humorous, they have a great value in helping faculty understand how their young students view the world. My own son was chastised by a teacher when he asked if he could hand out copies of a survey to his class as part of a science project. The teacher asked whether he had "run the survey off," to which he replied, "I guess so." Annoyed, she responded, "well, did you or didn't you? What is this 'I guess so?' routine?" My son then responded, "I don't know what 'run off' means."

To the teacher, who had undoubtedly run off many purple ditto sheets and stencil copies on Gestetner machines, the question was clear. To the student, an eighth grader who had never seen reproductions made by either method, the question was meaningless. What was interpreted as lack of respect and initiative was really a lack of ability to communicate because of different types of world experiences.

Gen Y in the Classroom

While Boomers like to be in charge of their own learning, and Gen Xers prefer to work independently with self-directed projects, Gen Y prefers learning that provides interaction with their colleagues. They like a lot more structure and direction than Generation X. They want to know **everything** up front as far as what is expected and what criteria will be used to evaluate their performance. They are the most likely to want to ask questions like, "Will this be on the test?" or specifics such as "how is this going to affect my life in a positive way?" Certainty and security is key for this group. Tying the learning outcomes to economic objectives that are important for Gen Y can also be important.

This generation is as comfortable with technology as a fish is with water. While older generations are intimidated, mystified or entranced by new technology, today's young adults will increasingly demand the applications of technology to learning as well as to work. An article in the February, 1999 issue of *Training* magazine, entitled "Get Ready for Generation Next" cautions: "If the technology used in [teaching] isn't state of the art, and if [instructors] don't know their stuff inside and out, the pupil may run circles around the master."

In spite of their technological savvy, Generation Y is in some ways very traditional. One study, conducted by Northwestern Mutual Life and the Harris organization found that college students in this generation felt the most affinity to their World War II-era grandparents and great-grandparents. Neil Howe, co-author of *13th Gen, The Fourth Turning,* and *Generations: The History of America's Future* has said that as workers, Gen Y will need more structure and attention from the authority figure than the preceding generation, Gen X. It is reasonable to assume that this is true also in the classroom, and current research suggests that this is the case.

Members of Gen Y are motivated to learn in order to reduce stress and increase their marketability. They place a high value on developing good interpersonal skills and in "getting along." This is a generation that is polite, believes in manners, adheres to a strict moral code, and believes in civic action.

This is a generation that places a high value on making money - more than any previous generation - and they see education as a means to this goal. Like Generation X, this generation likes learning to be entertaining and fun, and become quickly bored in a learning environment that is not highly active and interactive. They grew up with the Learning Channel and Chuck E. Cheese — edu-tainment and eat-o-tainment. Stand-up talking is deadly for this group who, even as adults, respond to music, art, games, and other creative activities (Zemke, et. al., 1999).

Learning materials for this group should have the same levels of visual interest and multiple focal points as those for Generation X. However, there is an important difference in Generation Y in this regard. It is a generation of readers, so written information works well for this group.

Tips for Teaching Gen Y

Some experts have asserted, "there is a growing mismatch between faculty and students in terms of teaching and learning" (Schroeder, 2004).

1. Develop opportunities for experiential learning. Small group discussions, projects, in-class presentations and debates, peer critiques, team projects, service learning, field experiences, developing simulations and case method approaches have been found to be successful for high school and college students (Schroeder, p. 9)

2. Encourage the development of learning communities—small groups of students that can discuss and analyze readings and assignments. This also addresses the need of many Gen Y students for hands-on activity in the classroom.

3. Provide lots of structure. Having grown up in a highly structured world, Gen Ys look for structure in their learning settings. They want to know precisely what is required of them, when work is due, and very specific information about expectations.

4. Provide lots of feedback. Providing frequent feedback is essential for Gen Ys. This allows them to know when they are headed in the right direction and when they are getting off-track. Frequent attention from teachers is welcome.

5. Use technology. This is a generation that uses technology for "everything." A classroom that does not incorporate it will not meet students' needs for variety, stimulation, and access to information. Some classrooms still require students to study and learn in ways that, to them, are completely different from the ways they operate in every other aspect of their daily lives.

6. Make it fun. Like their Gen X predecessors, Gen Ys want to enjoy their learning. If it is not fun, it will be cast into the category of "boring" and may become less effective. Millennials learn best when they are entertained.

7. Incorporate games. For Gen Y, using computer games as an instructional technique can be very effective. These incorporate many

of the strategies that Gen Ys have already developed for learning: multi-media sensory stimulation, interactivity (either with other people or with the computer), individualization (customization) of the learning experience, control over processing time, highly visual (Edel, 2004).

8. Be relevant. Like Gen Xers, Gen Ys will demand relevance in what they are learning. They will also want to "skip" steps in learning if there are areas of the information they have already mastered, and will avoid repetition and rote practice once they feel they have mastered the information.

9. Utilize their talents. This is a generation that likes to be useful and helpful. If you have students who know more about a topic than you do, let them talk about what they know. If they finish an assignment early, let them help other students.

10. Present the big picture. Many in this generation are global or "big picture" learners. They learn better if they have the big picture and then learn more concrete and specific information.

11. Allow for creativity and be creative. This is a generation that thinks in many dimensions at once. Provide opportunities for them to be creative in how they approach and fulfill requirements. Music, art, and games are good teaching tools.

12. Offer multiple options for performance. Try to provide a variety of acceptable, measurable outcomes so that students can optimize their performance.

13. Be visual. This group is the most visual of all learning cohorts. In general, visual learners predominate, but among Gen Y learners it is even more strongly preferred than in other age groups.

14. Be organized. Because they need a lot of structure, Gen Y students also learn best when materials are presented in a well-organized and rational way. Gen Y students are much more prolific readers than are Gen Xers, so reading materials for them are not a stumbling block. However, materials should be clear, use lots of white space, and be visually accessible, just as for Gen X. Summarizing key points to provide a point of reference for future learning tasks is very important for this group. They want to know where they are going with their learning… and why.

15. Be smart. Unlike Gen Xers, Gen Ys will not look at you with disdain if they feel they know more than you about a specific topic. However, they will expect you to be open to hearing their ideas and to demonstrate competence as a teacher. To this generation being "a good teacher" is more important than knowing everything.

16. Be fair. Like their Boomer parents, fairness is important to this group.

17. Recognize the need for social interaction. This is a key for Gen Y learners, so learning strategies that incorporate social interaction work well.

18 Remember, talk is essential. Develop activities that encourage students to exchange information verbally. When they say it, it is converted more quickly to long-term memory.

19. Structure a learning environment that demands respect and positive reinforcement. Positive reinforcement, from teachers and peers improves learning and increases motivation.

20. Tie learning to actions. For some key information, students can increase their recall if there is a specific action linked to the learning of a key fact. For example, if you want students to remember the date of the Norman invasion, when you give them the information, the year 1066, have them hold up 10 fingers and then 6 fingers. The information will stay with them forever.

21. Think positively. Positive thinking stimulates the brain. It increases the likelihood of success.

22. Be clear and precise. Give students clear goals, targets and purpose. Gen Y particularly wants to know precisely what they need to do to meet the requirements of the class. This is not a lack of intellectual curiosity, but a desire to be efficient. Keep in mind that these students have been exposed to more information in their lives than the two preceding generations combined. They know a lot. For them, school is one of many ways to get information, and they are used to getting what they need or want in ways that are efficient for them.

23. Allow focus time. The Gen Y attention span declines after 15-20 minutes. You have your student's brain for only 20 minutes at a time. Break up the class time into 20-30 minute segments with some other kind of activity (outbursts, e. g.).

24. Talk is critical. Talking stimulates the brain, in particular, the frontal lobe, the area which controls higher level thinking and decision making. Social interaction is important to memory and learning.
25. Enhance procedural memory with movement. Procedural memory is stored in the body—it is muscle memory. Riding a bike is an example of procedural memory. Procedural memory is easy to access. Relating procedural memory to cognitive tasks can improve recall.
26. Make learning relevant. Tie learning tasks to real-world problems. If it is not seen as relevant, there will be resistance to learning.

Chapter 13: A Pedagogy for the 21ˢᵗ Century

"In times of change, the learner will inherit the earth while the learned are beautifully equipped for a world that no longer exists."
— *Eric Hoffer* (*American philosopher, 1902-1983*)

There seems to be strong evidence that larger cultural issues impact the behavior and perceptions of people within different generations, and that this extends to learning as well as to other areas of life.

Since the 1980s, there has been a steady increase in the number of young men who graduate from high school and a steady decline in the number who choose to pursue education beyond high school, and that this decision is made well before the senior year. For example, the majority of students taking the ACT, a college entrance exam, are women. The participation of male high school students taking the ACT decreased from 52 percent of test takers in 1970 to 43 percent in 1998 ("Men and Women in Education").

While a great deal of attention has been focused recently on how schools are shortchanging boys, and had gained attention from the recent observations by First Lady, Laura Bush on how boys are being ill served (Borgman), this trend has been accelerating as the young adults of the 21ˢᵗ century progress through the education system.

a. By 2007 it is projected that women will make up 55 percent of full-time and 71 percent of part-time college students. (American Demographics, October, 1997).

129

b. The percent of all degrees conferred on men has decreased from 65.8 percent in 1960 to 44.2 percent in 1996 (116th Edition, Statistical Abstract of the United States (1966), the National Data Book of the U.S. Department of Commerce Statistics Administration).

These trends are noted here because they represent a growing crisis in the education system in the United States. It is discouraging to note that while the crisis began to unfold two and a half decades ago for boys, it has also begun to have a more profound impact upon girls. The following chart demonstrates how students feel about their educational experiences. We have long heard the cries of dismay that the "schools are failing our kids," but we have seen no move to embrace a pedagogy that serves today's young learners.

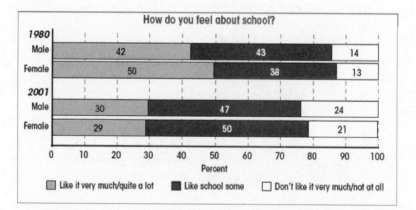

National Center for Education Statistics, Trends in Educational Equity of Girls and Women 2004 http://nces.ed.gov/pubs2005/equity/ Section12.asp

Clearly, the dissatisfaction with school, while greater for male students, is also having an impact upon girls as well. The solution is to vigorously pursue a new pedagogy that is appropriate for 21st century learners.

Such pedagogy should include the following components:

Learner Centered

For the first time in the memory of Baby Boomers, the term "progressive" was used in the last presidential campaign. Just as a progressive movement emerged in the early years of the 20th century, such a movement is stirring in the 21st Century. One of the hallmarks of the progressive movement in education was the development of a learner-centered curriculum. The concept was to create for the learners a curriculum that accounted for learning, play, and work. The curriculum further took into account the changing nature of society, and the transition from farm to industry as the main economic base. Just as young men are abandoning school today, young men in the early 20th century dropped out in large numbers. They found more satisfaction working in the factory than in the classroom. In fact, it was not the compulsory education laws that contributed to the increase in educational attainment in the early 1900s. It was the passage of child labor laws that made it illegal for young people to work in the factory.

In today's world, there are parallels. Young men are abandoning education because it is less relevant to them than is the larger world. Further, in today's education system, the curriculum is almost completely learner-centered in the primary grades. In the middle and high school grades, it becomes increasingly subject-centered, and it is precisely at this point where students begin to fail in larger numbers. Creating a learner-centered curriculum and learning environment is an important key to teaching effectively in the 21st century.

On college campuses, there is a trend in this direction for entering freshmen. Most campuses have a structured freshman experience that focuses very heavily on the learner, is critical to creating success in subsequent years, and in increasing persistence toward earning a degree.

Collaborative, not Competitive

Today's youth are team players, understand the value of working together, and recognize that in a collaborative environment the learning outcomes are enhanced for all participants.

Relevant

When we speak of relevance here, we do not mean that the learning experience should merely be relevant to the somewhat artificial goal of graduation or GPA. These goals are still important, but they are not the motivators for learning that they were for learners in previous generations. The goal for younger learners is to learn information that can be put to practical use. If there is not clear relationship between usefulness and learning, motivation will drop. Understanding relevance is essential to motivation.

Time Appropriate

For today's young learners, time is the most important commodity. The value of time is foremost. Students will evaluate the time it takes to complete an assignment, the number of "points" to be earned and the value of the information. If either the value of the information or the number of points earned by spending the time to do an assignment is not clear, students will not devote their time to the work. Time is scarce, hard to come by, and not to be spent frivolously. Further, if information is relevant, students will generally find time to learn it, but they may take shortcuts, not "complete" the assignment, or otherwise fail to meet teachers' expectations. This is especially true for male students.

Outcomes Based

For today's students, outcomes are more important than process in terms of learning. Students will focus on areas where they may need to improve, and skip or ignore entirely material they already know. This means, again, assignments not completed or only partially completed. In most cases, students will be satisfied with good results on tests and evaluations, and less diligent about pre-determined processes for learning the information.

It is important to remember that today's students have had access to incredible amounts of information from birth - more by age five than their great grandparents experienced in a lifetime. They have learned strategies for sorting information, internalizing what is of value or use, and processing huge amounts of input with a speed and sense of organization that most adults today cannot fathom.

Customized

This is the age of mass customization. Today's youth have always been able to customize their world. A recent commercial on television focuses on a mother who customizes the soup her children eat: crackers for one, mixed with milk for another, a few veggies added for a third, and so on. Today's learners need to be able to customize, to some degree, how they learn required information, and ideally there should be a variety of evaluation methods to measure learning.

Interactive

Today's students often learn best when their learning experiences are interactive. If they are learning face to face, interacting with peers and teachers is important. In some schools, teachers are increasing the use of technology in their classes. Some schools we know of even have teacher "blogs" where students can engage in dialogue with each other and faculty members relative to issues of importance in various course areas.

Incorporate Technology

Many of today's students were using computers before they could walk or talk. The medium of interactive technology has become important as a tool in their learning, and moving into a traditional classroom of lecture and note taking is like shifting from talkies back to silent film. It won't work very well.

Visual

Today's youth are the most visual of all learners. While it is important to cultivate a variety of learning styles, the permeation of society by visual media will continue to impact learners, and many will learn best in this modality. In addition, young learners are expert at scanning and identifying important information, so clear visual presentation is important.

Clear Expectations

Both Gen X and Gen Y want to have expectations clearly stated and outcomes defined. This is an essential element because they will develop their own learning strategies (which may or may not follow traditional teaching practice). They are focused on the end result, not the process for getting there.

Summary

Human beings have been trying, for thousands of years, to understand the nature of learning and knowing. There are many different instruments for measuring how individuals learn best, and many different kinds of preferences that these instruments measure. One problem that persists, even when an individual's learning style is determined by a valid instrument, is that even when people have the same learning style preferences, they don't necessarily learn "best" in the same kind of setting or from the same techniques.

One consideration, which is often overlooked, is that of "cultural" relevance. Learners from different generations, in effect, have grown up in different cultures. They have different values, different expectations, and even speak, to some degree, different languages. These factors all have critical relevance in a learning setting. While there is still much debate about the value of matching teaching styles to learning styles, it seems more apparent that there is great value in matching teaching strategies to generational- based learning styles.

Summary of Generational Characteristics

Baby Boomers
- Re-defined roles
- Promoted equality
- Sought immediate gratification
- Manipulated rules to fit their situation

Core Values
- Optimistic
- Team oriented
- Seek personal gratification
- Obsessed with health and wellness
- Pursue personal growth and self-understanding
- Youthful oriented
- Work hard/driven to succeed
- Involved in community/family
- Willing to go the extra mile
- Want to please
- Service oriented

Boomers are not:
- Budget minded.
- Comfortable with conflict.
- Comfortable going against peers.
- Tolerant of those who see things differently.

Boomers are:
- Self-centered.
- May put process ahead of outcome.

Messages that Motivate
- You are important to our success.
- You are valued.
- Your contribution is unique and important.
- We need you.
- I approve of you.
- You're worthy.

In the classroom you should:
- Value their experience.
- Challenge them to make a difference.
- Show them how to excel/be a star.
- Give lots of positive feedback.

In the classroom, Boomers:
- Like to be creative and independent.
- Don't like authority.
- Like collegial atmosphere.
- Like ice-breakers and introductions.
- Know a lot and like to share.
- Require a lot of "talk time."
- Are sensitive to criticism.
- Want time to practice new skills.
- Like materials to be organized with major headings and information below.
- Like team/group activities.
- Don't like to role play.

Marketing

- Down-age marketing messages.
- Boomers think they are 15 to 20 years younger than they are.
- Focus on experience or product, not age.
- Emphasize comfort, convenience, quality.
- Develop messages that appeal to core values.

Generation X

Core Values

- Diversity
- Thinking globally
- Balance
- Technoliteracy
- Fun
- Informality
- Self-reliance
- Pragmatism

Gen Xers are:

- Adaptable.
- Technoliterate.
- Independent.
- Unintimidated by authority.
- Creative.
- Impatient.

and

- May have poor interpersonal skills.
- May lack experience.
- May seem cynical or negative.

In the classroom, Gen Xers:

- Want all the facts at the outset.
- Need to exactly what expectations are.
- Are impatient with rote/busy work or work that seems irrelevant.
- Don't automatically respect expertise of the teacher.
- Are intolerant of instructors who can't use technology.
- Want to know the relevance of everything they are expected to learn.
- Very visual.
- Need to see how the learning will help them get ahead.
- Need to be convinced that your class is more important than anything else they might be doing in their "spare" time.

In the classroom, you should:

- Provide materials with lots of white space and bullet points.
- Put all the relevant information up front. They won't read for details.
- Put information online.
- Be as brief as possible to communicate what is needed.
- Not try to sugarcoat your instructions or information.
- Be direct and accurate about your expectations.
- Not micro-manage. Tell them what to do, not how they should do it—unless they ask.
- Use humor.

Marketing
- Very media savvy
- Not responsive to "spin"
- Will buy for quality. Brand is less important
- Quality is most important (value for dollar)
- Don't want any messages sugarcoated or "softened"
- Want information to be humorous, even edgy
- Demand good design and graphics, color

Gen Y
Core Values
- Optimism
- Civic duty
- Confidence
- Achievement
- Sociability
- Morality
- Street smarts
- Diversity

In the classroom, Gen Y:
- Is collaborative.
- Is tenacious.
- Can multi-task.
- Is technologically savvy.
- Needs supervision and structure.
- Is inexperienced.
- Has trouble with difficult people issues.
- Is very visual.
- Tends to be kinesthetic (hands on) learners.

- Needs lots of visual stimulation.
- Humor helps.
- Demands relevance.
- May know more than the teacher about many things.
- Is willing to help other students as well as the instructor.
- Needs very specific understandings of expectations spelled out — 1, 2, 3, etc.

In the classroom, you should:
- Be very specific.
- Avoid direct criticism which may be taken personally.
- Be collaborative, not directive.
- Ask for help if you can't work the LCD... or use the software... or make the Powerpoint presentation run properly...
- Recognize that students may not ask for help... or know how to.
- Provide opportunities for interaction and collaborative learning with other students (NOT just group "projects").
- Provide brief changes of pace about every 20 minutes to assist with processing and assimilation of information. (This works with all age groups, but is especially important for Gen Y.)
- Provide learner-centered, multisensory teaching strategies.

Marketing
- Most media savvy of all the generations
- Least responsive to marketing efforts
- Viral marketing (word of mouth) is very important
- Trust each other and will check out the value of a product before buying, even if they have seen an ad. Lots of marketing with Gen Y is "two-step" marketing, i.e., awareness and then confirmation.
- Demand good graphics, contemporary images, color
- Humor, fun, goofiness work

References

All Things Considered, National Public Radio. February 9, 2004.

America at school: motion pictures from 1894-1915. Library of Congress Motion Picture, Broadcasting and Recorded Sound Division Washington, D.C. Retrieved on November 16, 2005 from http://memory.loc.gov/ammem/awlhtml/awlscho.html.

Borgman, L. "Girls Excel but Boys Need Nurture Too." Retrieved from http://www.crosswalk.com/family/1314754.html on October 3, 2005.

Bowser, Eileen. (1994) *The Transformation of Cinema, 1907-1915. History of the American Cinema, (2).* Berkeley: University of California Press.

Carpenter, E. and McLuhan, M. eds. (1960). *Explorations in communication: An anthology.* Boston: Beacon Press as quoted in University of Toronto Explorations #6, pp. 15-19. Retrieved from http://66.102.7.104/search?q=cache:dXB_62VaC-wJ:ccins.camosun.bc.ca/~pculture/mcluhan/mc_41.txt+McLuhan+%22Before+print+the+community+at+large%22&hl=en on December 7, 2005.

Claxton, C. S., & Ralston, Y. (1978*). Learning styles: Their impact on teaching and administration.* Washington, DC: American Association for Higher Education.

Dewey and Lippman: A Comparison: Chapter 3. Powerpoint presentation. Retrieved from http:www.cwrl.utexas.edu/~longaker/rhe330e/DeweyLippmannComparison3.ppt#260,5, Slide 5, on December 7, 2005.

Digest of Education Stastics Tables and Figures (2003). National Center for Education Statistics. Accessed from http://nces.ed.gov/programs/digest/d03/index.asp on October 5, 2005.

Cohen, R. D. (2002). *Children of the mill: Schooling and society in Gary, Indiana.* London: RoutledgeFalmer Press.

Demasio, A. (1995). *Descartes' Error,* 90-201. NY: Harper Perennial.

Dewey, J. (1901). *The child and the curriculum.* Mineola: Dover Publications.

Dewey, J. (1906). *Democracy and Education.* NY: Mcmillan Company.

Dunn, Rita S. (1996). *How to implement and supervise a learning style program.* Baltimore: Association for Supervision & Curriculum Development.

Edel, M. (2004). "Learning Tools for the New Generation," presentation at ITeach 2004: *Best Practices in Teaching with Technology Annual Conference,* Hennepin Technical College, Brooklyn Park, April 15 – 17.

Encarta. Public Education in the United States. Retrieved November 14, 2005 from http://encarta.msn.com/encyclopedia_761571494/ Public_Education_in_the_United_States.html.

Felder, R.M. (1993). Reaching the second tier: Learning and teaching styles in college science education. *Journal of College Science Teaching, 23(5),* 286-290.

Felder, R. M. & Silverman, L.K. (1998). Learning and Teaching Styles in Engineering Education. *Engr. Education, 78*(7), 674-681. Retrieved June 12, 2005 from http://www.ncsu.edu/felder-public/Papers/LS-1988.pdf.

Fishbaugh, M.S.E. (2000, July). One Room Schools in Montana at the Turn of the Century 1999-2001. Paper presented at the International Special Education Congress, Retrieved on September, 2005 from http:// www.isec2000.org.uk/abstracts/papers_f/fishbaugh_1.htm. University of Manchester.

Follett, M. P. (1918). *The new state.* Chapter 27: From neighborhood to nation: The unifying state. Full text available at http://sunsite.utk.edu/ FINS/Mary_Parker_Follett/Fins-MPF-01.html.

Gardner, H. (1993). *Frames of Mind: the theory of multiple intelligences.* NY: BasicBooks.

Hanks, L.B. (1996). *Vision, variety and vitality: Teaching today's adult generations.* Nashville, Convention Press.

Hornblower, M. (1997). "Great Xpectations." *Time.* June 9: 58-68.

Hornblower, M. (1997). "Great Xpectations." *Time.* June 9: 58-68.

Horvitz, L. & Larson D. (Directors). (1998). Dreams do come true [Recorded by Jackson Browne]. In *The Wizard of Oz in Concert Soundtrack* [Motion Picture]. US: Turner Home Video.

Hyman, I. A. & Perone, D.C. (1998). The other side of school violence. *Journal of School Psychology (36)* 1, pp 7-27.

Jensen, E. (1998). *Teaching with the brain in mind.* pp 1-2, 45-47, 63-35, Alexandria, VA: Association for Supervision and Curriculum Development (ASCD).

Johnsen, Julia E. (1925). *Child Labor.* pp 144-145. NY: The H.W. Wilson Company.

Hicks, Rosie and Gable, Karen. The learning style profile of Indiana's secondary health Occupation students. *Journal of Health Occupations Education 13(1),* 9.

Keefe, J. W. (1979). Learning style: An overview. In NASSP's Student learning styles: diagnosing and prescribing programs (pp. 1-17). Reston, VA: National Association of Secondary School Principals.

Keefe, J. W., & Languis, M. L. (1983). Operational definitions. Paper presented to the National Association of Secondary School Principals Learning Styles Task Force.

Kismaric, C. and Heiferman, M. (1996) *Growing up with Dick and Jane: Learning and living the American dream.* NY: Harper Paperbacks; BK & Acces edition.

Outlook '96 (January 2, 1996). *New York Times.*

Reston, VA. James W. Keefe, Editor. Reston, VA: NASSP.

Knowles, M. S. (1973; 1990) *The adult learner. A neglected species* (4e), Houston: Gulf Publishing.

LeRoy, M. (Producer) & Fleming, V. (Director). (1939). *The Wizard of Oz* [Motion Picture]. United States: Metro-Goldwyn Mayer.

Martin, V. (2002). ADHD: Fact, fiction and beyond: A comprehensive study of attention deficit hyperactivity disorder. Retrieved November 15, 2004 from http://adhdtexas.com/history.htm.

McLuhan M. (1967). *The medium is the massage.* NY: Bantam Books.

"Men and Women in Education." Gender Issues Research Center. Retrieved from http://www.gendercenter.org/education.htm on December 9, 2005.

Mondale, S. (2002). *School: The story of American public education.* Boston: Beacon Press.

Mortenson, T. G. (2000). Chronicle of Higher Education Colloquy Live, November 1, 2000. Retrieved from http://chronicle.com/colloquylive/transcripts/2000/11/20001101kingmort.htm on December 8, 2005.

NASSP National Task Force (1993). National task force defines learning style operationally and conceptually. *National styles network newsletter, 4(21).* National Association of Secondary School Principals and St. John's University.

Ontario Secondary School Teachers Federation. (2001). Ten things wrong with high stakes testing. Retrieved October 18, 2004 from http://www.osstf.on.ca/archives/dept/edu/ssr/tenthings.html.

Ouellette, R. (2000). Learning Styles in adult education. Web initiatives in teaching conference. Retrieved November 14, 2005 from http://polaris.umuc.edu/~rouellet/learnstyle/index.htm.

Parker, D.B. (1994). The rise and fall of *The Wonderful Wizard of Oz* as a parable on populism. *Journal of the Georgia Association of Historians, 15,* 49-63. Retrieved on November 16, 2005 from http://www.halcyon.com/piglet/Populism.htm.

Pipher, M. (1996). *The shelter of each other.* NY: Ballentine Books.

Pipher, M. (1998). Engaging parents and the community in schools in *Educational Leadership (55)* 8, pp. 6-11.

Putnam, R. (2000). *Bowling alone,* pp. 246-281, 300-380. NY: Touchstone.

Putnam, R. (2000). *Bowling alone,* p. 273. NY: Touchstone.

Putnam, R. (2000). *Bowling alone,* p. 264. NY: Touchstone.

Putnam, R. (2000). *Bowling alone,* pp. 257-260. NY: Touchstone.

Putnam, R. (2000). *Bowling alone,* p. 283. NY: Touchstone.

Putnam, R. (2000). *Bowling alone,* p. 256. NY: Touchstone.

Putnam, R. (2000). *Bowling alone,* p. 298. NY: Touchstone.

Putnam, R. (2000). *Bowling alone,* p. 302. NY: Touchstone.

Putnam, R. (2000). *Bowling alone,* pp. 377-378. NY: Touchstone.

Putnam, R. (2000). *Bowling alone,* pp. 386-389. NY: Touchstone.

Resnick, M. and Jablokov, A. (1998). Nostalgia [Edited version of a discussion held at MIT on November 19, 1998]. Retrieved from http://web.mit.edu/m-i-t/science_fiction/transcripts/resnick_jablokov.html on April 16, 2003.

Rezler, A., & Rezmovic, V. (1981). The learning preference inventory. *Journal of Applied Health,* 10(1), 28-34.

Roosevelt, T. (1907). Letter to Cuno H. Rudolph, Washington Playground Association. Presidential Addresses and State Papers VI, 1163. Retrieved from http://www.theodoreroosevelt.org/life/quotes.htm on December 7, 2005.

Schroeder, C. (2004), "New Students—New Learning Styles." Retrieved from "New http://www.virtualschool.edu/mon/Academia/ KierseyLearningStyles.html on October 7, 2005.

Strauss, W. and Howe, N. (1997). *The Fourth Turning.* NY: Broadway Books.

Streep, M. (Narrator). PBS Series, *School: The story of American public education* (2001). Information available at http://www.pbs.org/kcet/ publicschool/about_the_series/index.html.

Sylwester, R. (1995a). *A celebration of neurons: An educator's guide to the human brain,* pp 77-84,. Alexandria: Association for Supervision and Curriculum Development (ASCD).

TePas, T. E. (1996). Attention deficit/hyperactivity disorder revisited. *NOHA news, XXI* (4), pp 3-6. Retrieved on August 12, 2005 from http:// www.nutrition4health.org/NOHAnews/NNF96ADHD.htm.

Tessmer, M. & Jonassen, D.H. (1988). Learning strategies: A new instructional technology. In N.D.C. Harris (Ed.), World yearbook of education: Education for the new technologies. London: Kogan Page.

Tobias, Sheila. (1990). They're not dumb, they're different: Stalking the second tier. Tucson, Research Corporation.

Trends in Educational Equity of Girls and Women 2004 National Center for Education Statistics, available at http://nces.ed.gov/pubs2005/equity/ Section12.asp.

United States census bureau statistical abstract of the United States. (1999). Twentieth century statistics. No. 1425. Education summary—enrollment, graduates, and degrees: 1900 to 1998, and projections 1999 and 2000. Retrieved November 14, 2005 from http://www.census.gov/prod/99pubs/ 99statab/sec31.pdf.

Warren, B.Z. & Dziuban, C.C. (1997) Personality, learning-style, gender and ethnic charactistics of students attending supplemental instruction in spring of 1997 at the University of Central Florida. Presented at the Annual Teaching/Learning Conference, Ashland, Kentucky.

Welfare and Marriage (March 13, 2002). Morning Edition, National Public Radio.

We Work and Play (1946). pp 9, 14. New York: Scott Foresman & Company.

WGBH Radio (Producer). Kushner, E. (Host). Nostalgia on *Sound and Spirit*. Public Radio International, 1999. Retrieved from http:// www.wgbh.org/pages/pri/spirit/alphabetical.html and http://www.wgbh.org/ pages/pri/spirit/shows/080bibl.html on November 18, 2005.

Wichman, J. (2000). Happy mellow school pill: Paying attention to the ritalin debate. *Shepherd Express Metro: Health Watch (21)* 36. Retrieved on November 27, 2004 from http://ads.newcitynet.com/RealMedia/ads/ click.cgi/www.shepherd-express.com/shepherd/21/36/index.html?85,58.

Williams, G. (2000). Lost generation and found generation: introducing the generation called Jones. *Entrepreneur* May, 2000. Retrieved October 12, 2005 from http://www.entrepreneur.com/mag/article/ 0,1539,271536,00.html.

Zemke, R., Raines, C., Filipczak, B. (2000). *Generations at work: Managing the clash of veterans, boomers, xers and nexters in your workplace,* pp. 3, 99, NY: American Management Association.

Zemke, R., Raines, C., Filipczak, B. (2000). *Generations at work: Managing the clash of veterans, boomers, xers and nexters in your workplace,* pp. 29-30, NY: American Management Association.

Zemke, R., Raines, C., Filipczak, B. (1999). Generation Gaps in the Company Classroom, *Training* Magazine. Retrieved February 3, 2004 from http://www.millennials.com/Training99.html.

Bibliography

Calvin, William H., The Throwing Madonna, Bantam, 1991.

Gurian, Michael, Boys and Girls Learn Differently: A Guide for Teachers and Parents, Jossey-Bass, 2001.

Knowles, Malcolm, The Modern Practice of Adult Education: Pedagogy vs Androgogy, New York, Association Press, 1970.

Sternberg, Robert J., Thinking Styles, Cambridge University Press, 1997.

Zemke, Ron, et. al, Generations at Work, AMACOM, 2000.

Online Learning Styles Resources

www.bizresources.com/learning/de_deskguide.html

www.instructordiploma.com/core/102%20B/Sandra.htm

http://home.earthlink.net/~dadidpdiaz/LTShtml_docs/grslss.htm

http://www.technos.net/journal/volume10/1greenberg.htm

http://dino.tafe.sa.edu.au/lsrsc/one/natproj/tal/survey/index.htm

http://home.earthlink.net/~daviddiaz/LTS/html_docs/newpath.htm

ERIC Sources

EJ193745. Brown, Ric. The Effects of Congruency between Learning Style and Teaching Style on College Student Achievement. College Student Journal; v12 n3 p307-09 Fall 1978. 1978

ED228235. Cornett, Claudia E.. What You Should Know About Teaching and Learning Styles. Fastback 191. . 1983

EJ560445. Spoon, Jerry C.; Schell, John W.. Aligning Student Learning Styles with Instructor Teaching Styles. Journal of Industrial Teacher Education; v35 n2 p41-56 Win 1998. 1998

ED171752. Scerba, John R.. Compatibility of Teaching Strategies and Learning Styles as a Determinant of Academic Success. . 1979

ED340506. Reiff, Judith C.. Learning Styles. What Research Says to the Teacher Series. . 1992

ED172635. Blue, Terry W.. Teaching and Learning Styles in Higher Education: Match or Mismatch? . 1979

ED222477. Semple, Edward E., Jr.. Learning Style. A Review of the Literature. . 1982

EJ311744. Heikkinen, Michael; And Others. Learning Styles vs. Teaching Styles—Studying the Relationship. NASSP Bulletin; v69 n478 p80-85 Feb 1985. 1985

ED208263. Lapides, Jerry. Teaching Styles in Adult Education. An Exploratory Essay. 1980

About LERN

The Learning Resources Network (LERN) is the leading association in the world in lifelong learning programming, serving more than 10,000 professionals every year in 20 countries.

Begun in 1974, LERN offers information and consulting to providers of lifelong learning programs, including for-profit and non-profit organizations, such as universities, community colleges, public schools, recreation departments, training providers, associations and others.

LERN provides practical, how-to information on marketing, finances, management, product development, teaching and course design. It is information not available anywhere else.

A specialty area of expertise is online learning and teaching, with LERN being the leading provider of online professional development for faculty and teachers using the Internet.

LERN is a nonprofit, tax-exempt, educational organization. We are led by a Board of Directors, with daily operations carried out by a staff and consultants located in eight states. With a mission to extend lifelong learning to all, our slogan is "Information That Works!" ®

For More About Generational Learning Styles

Online Course: Generational Learning Styles.
  One week asynchronous online course. With this one-week, online course, you will learn more about your students, and discover something new about your own learning style. For trainers, teachers, faculty, human resource professionals and others interested in learning.

Keynotes and Speaking
  For your next conference or meeting, book a Generational Learning Styles speaker and get information not available anywhere else. Julie Coates and her associates present a lively slide show and customized presentation that gets rave review from audiences.

On-site In-House seminars
  Bring Generational Learning Styles to your organization. Customized practical how-to seminars are available on generational communication in the workplace, generational marketing, and other topics related to generational learning styles.

Four Day Institute
  Get the most comprehensive and intensive training available on generational learning styles. Julie Coates and her associates present a four day institute for professionals.

For the latest information on Generational Learning Styles:
www.GenerationalLearningStyles.com

For questions, book a speaker or register.
Contact us at:
Email: info@lern.org
Call: 800-678-5376 or 715-426-9777 (8-5 Central time weekdays)
URL: www.lern.org